SET FREE

SOARING BEYOND LIMITS

FITH FITHIAN

I would like to acknowledge and express my gratitude to my friends and family, both past and present. Friends are like tree branches; some flourish for a season and then pass, while other principal branches last a lifetime. I may have said goodbye to past friends, but nonetheless, they have helped direct me to where I am today. As for family, they are always there and need no further explanation. Finally, I give all the credit to the big guy upstairs. John 3:16.

I hope you enjoy the book,

UNCLE FISH.

*I dedicate this book to all those I love,
and you know who you are.*

Never regret thy fall, O Icarus of the fearless flight. For the greatest tragedy of them all is never to feel the burning light.

-OSCAR WILDE-

TABLE OF CONTENTS

CHAPTER ONE

Weaving in and out of the trees and kicking up dirt, Cody cruised off the ramp his dad had helped him build when he first picked up mountain biking.

His legs had quickly outgrown the rest of him, earning him the nickname "Cody Long Legs" when he was only five years old. When he got on his first mountain bike that same year, a beat-up orange, black, and white Huffy, the embarrassment of the name no longer mattered. His legs were his superpower. Now, at ten, Cody was prepping for his first youth downhill race.

The outdoors was where Cody felt the most comfortable. It was his place of escape, a refuge from the busy world at school and home. After Cody made a few more laps on the small track he'd set for racing his friends, he leaned his Huffy against the tree to run in and grab some water.

From inside, Cody heard the quiet, muffled chirp of the parakeets his mom and dad loved having in the house. The sound brought Cody's original plan straight back to the front of his mind.

He snatched the blanket off the cage, revealing the two bright yellow parakeets he had grown to know and love. Staring at these birds brought up a sense of longing and desire that he struggled to put into words for his parents to understand. Setting the birds free was more of a need than a simple desire that Cody dreamt of throughout the day.

Quickly, Cody peeked out the window, checking for any sign that his parents might have come home early. Once he was satisfied that he was alone, he bounded down the steps back to his two yellow friends in their cage.

Cody had opened the cage and taken both the birds out to play before, but this time was going to be different. He unlatched the door and took them delicately into his hands.

"Say goodbye to your prison, little birdies. The world is yours now," Cody whispered softly enough that he was surely the only one to hear.

Outside, he set them on a branch underneath the treehouse he played in every single day since his dad had built it for him when he was nine. He loved this place so deeply that he knew the birds would too.

The birds simply sat there, staring right back at Cody. The confusion would have been obvious to any observers, if there were any.

"Go on! Don't you understand? You're free!"

Cody shooed the birds off their branch, forcing them into flight. They took a few steps along the branch and hopped over to a new one, seemingly unable to take the full leap to freedom.

This time, Cody channeled his most directive voice and said to the birds, "Go ahead, little birdies! Fly! Get on out of here!"

The birds leaped off the branch, more out of shock than anything. This ten-year-old boy had only ever shown them love. Now, he seemed angry, shouting at the birds to go. Whether it was fear or forceful love that did it, Cody would never know, but the birds took off into the sky.

He watched as they fluttered past his treehouse into the canopy of the towering spruce, fur, and pine trees he had grown up playing in. Slowly, the birds got smaller and smaller until he could no longer make them out amongst the swaying branches of the trees around them.

Cody didn't want his parents to know it was he who had set these birds off to a better life, so he ran inside before his mom could get home from work and catch him in the act. He slammed the cage door shut and threw the blanket back on top of it, attempting to make it look as if no one had touched it that day.

To make it all seem a bit more natural, he ran to his treehouse refuge and began scrambling up the massive ladder toward the trap door that let him in. Halfway up the ladder, Cody paused to look out and see if his parakeet friends had tried to come back home. Seeing nothing but the leaves of the trees rustling in the wind, he was satisfied that they had found a new perch.

Cody scrambled up through the trap door and went immediately to his secret stash of snacks. He reached for his favorite, a candy bar he had been saving since last Halloween. This seemed like a time to celebrate.

It had taken Cody's dad a year to build this treehouse for Cody's ninth birthday. He wanted to create a space where Cody could get out, feel independent, and live amongst the trees. He had seen the spark in Cody's eyes when he went outside, even at a young age. Building a treehouse had felt like a small thing to do to keep that spark alive.

This home amongst the trees was more than a few old planks of wood thrown up with some nails and glue. This refuge was built to live in with electricity, functioning glass windows, and a hatch door that locked securely enough to keep any curious bear on the outside. Ever since his dad finished building the fort, Cody spent almost as many nights sleeping out there as he did inside the house.

Aside from his treehouse, Cody had his bike. With these two things, he could stay happy forever.

With his feet kicked up and his body slowly sinking into the treehouse's beanbag, Cody popped open the window and took in the world around him. He thought about how depressing it would be to be trapped inside at all times. He could feel the pain, not only imagine it. He felt as if a massive weight had come off his shoulders now that his parakeet friends were no longer trapped in a cage, unable to fully spread their wings.

Cody had spent what seemed like a lifetime sitting in this exact spot, dreaming of flying. Birds flew by the window and often landed on the sill, giving him a brief moment to sit in awe and imagine a life in which he could launch himself through the sky with nothing to worry about.

A tickling on his arm alerted him to a large green caterpillar making its way toward his shoulder. He gently scooped the caterpillar into his hands and brought it up close to his eyes. He grabbed the magnifying glass that was always within arm's reach and examined the caterpillar closely.

"One day, you'll get to fly. Just be patient, little guy."

He set it down on a leaf in the tree next to the window, and the caterpillar immediately began to eat.

Just as Cody was imagining himself forming a small cocoon, preparing to fly, the sound of his mom's car pulled him back to the present. Immediately he was nervous she would know he let the birds out.

To act normal, Cody slid down his escape slide and ran to greet his mom. Before Cody could make it to her, she was already on his case about leaving the front door open.

"Cody! We live in the middle of the forest! I don't know what I'd do if I came home to a black bear rifling through the fridge!"

"I know, Mom. I'm sorry. But wouldn't it be cool if the bear came and made us dinner?" Cody replied, instantly regretting coming out of his treehouse.

His mom let out a long sigh. "I've told you a million times. The door needs to stay shut. We can't have all the woodland creatures come in and start expecting fresh fish in the fridge."

"Even if I took care of them?"

"Yes, honey. Even then. Now grab the eggs out of the front seat and help me put these groceries away."

His mom could be tough on him sometimes, but Cody's dad always assured him that it came from all the love she had for him. It sure didn't feel that way at times.

As Cody absent-mindedly walked into the kitchen, he heard some chirping from above, reminding him of the birds he had just set free. A good reminder to act normal.

"Cody Robert McCully! Close that dang door behind you, or I'll have you dressed up as a bellhop with no choice but to stand there and do nothing but close it!"

"Yes, ma'am," Cody replied as he whipped around to shut the door.

"Hey, Cody…where are the birds?"

Cody froze in place. His mom must have followed her ritual of unpacking groceries and then immediately feeding the birds.

Slowly, Cody turned around to face his mother.

"The birds? I don't know; I thought I heard them this morning. But they have been awfully quiet. I've been up in my treehouse. Why?" He tried to put a convincing sense of confusion and curiosity into his voice, unsure if she would buy it.

"You didn't happen to…let them out, did you?"

Cody tried to put on his best surprised face, but he could only imagine she saw pure guilt. "What! No way! I would never do that."

With an obvious sense of disbelief, Cody's mom looked him up and down as she slowly walked toward where he was standing.

"How about you head up to your room with your cereal and wait until your dad gets home? Maybe up there, you'll be able to figure out what happened to the birds," she said with what Cody perceived as a menacing tone.

"But, Mom! I want to go back outside!"

"Go, Cody. Before I have to tell you again."

Cody took his box of Lucky Charms cereal and bolted upstairs to wait for his dad to get home.

Cody stared out of his bedroom window, hoping he would see the yellow feathers of the parakeets flutter by so he would know they were safe, but he saw nothing. The blue skies were beautiful, but he was looking for something else.

Along with a sudden crisp breeze of air, one of the parakeets fluttered in and landed immediately in front of Cody on his windowsill. The bird cocked its head and stared directly at him as he stared right back.

"I don't care if I get in trouble. You're obviously happier than I am, stuck up here in my room."

He nudged the bird back off the windowsill, encouraging it to fly back out to the world. The parakeet seemed to resist, but eventually took flight and was out of sight before Cody could register what just happened.

"One day, I'll be able to get away. I'll fly away, just like you." He recited the quiet vow he always made to the birds flying by his window.

He watched the bird fly back and forth across the open air and pictured himself flying next to the bird. Sleep crept closely in as he sat daydreaming until the rumbling of his dad's old Ford Ranger jolted him back to this world.

The rattling siren on top of his dad's truck made it impossible to miss. Once it rolled into view, the forest green Park Ranger logo made it even more unmistakably his. Cody loved that truck, but today it was a sign of him getting into trouble, so he ran to hide underneath the covers. He always pretended his covers could be a shield to hide him from the trouble his shenanigans got him into. Even though it never seemed to work, he kept on trying.

Rex McCully, dressed in his park ranger uniform, walked towards the front door with his lunch bag in one hand and truck keys swinging in the other. Even with his slight limp, he always gave off a rugged yet peaceful aura everywhere he went.

Without a word, Rex gently kissed his wife on the cheek, even before setting anything down.

"Good evening, my love," he recited with a sense of routine that hadn't lost its importance.

Nicole McCully showed an obvious sign of comfort from the moment her husband walked in the door. Her entire demeanor shifted with his presence, allowing her to smile at her husband of ten years.

"How was work?" she asked, giving him her full attention.

"Long, but I wouldn't have it any other way," Rex replied. "The harder days just mean that the park needs me more than usual, and I'm happy to protect it. How was your day?"

Nicole handed Rex a cup of coffee before launching into her report of Cody's behavior. The two of them shared a brief moment of silence before bringing up the necessities.

"You'll need to go talk to Cody. He finally let the parakeets out this afternoon, just like we worried he would," she informed him with a feeling of relief and tension.

"He did what now?"

"That's right. He let those parakeets out into the forest. Probably hoping they would just go live in his treehouse with him. He meant no harm, I'm sure. Probably just wanted them to be free."

"And did you tell him that not all animals are meant to be free?"

"You know he'll hear it better coming from you, Rex."

"Alright, alright, I'll head up," he said, taking a final swig of coffee, seemingly for courage, and headed up toward Cody's room.

When he arrived at the door, he heard nothing but silence, meaning Cody knew he was on his way. As he opened the door, he thought to himself, *Just play the game; it'll go smoother that way.*

He walked across the room toward the closet, acting oblivious. To make a show of searching for his son, he avoided the blanket that Cody was under and called out, "Cody! Where arrrre you? I know you're in here!"

With a dramatic flair, he opened the closet door, shouting, "Gotcha!"

From behind him, he heard a snicker coming from underneath the blanket.

"Aha! You can't hide from me!" he shouted toward Cody as he ran over and began tickling the blanket.

Cody writhed around in laughter while simultaneously asking his dad to stop. "Okay, okay! You found me!" he gasped out between spurts of uncontrollable laughter.

Cody's dad let up on the tickling and swooped Cody into his arms to move him to the side of the bed. After a few moments of calm, he finally asked, "Cody, did you let the birds out of the cage?"

The silence in the room was deafening as Cody played around with different ideas of how to respond. He'd been thinking about it since his dad's truck pulled up, but he still had no clue what the right thing to say was.

As if he could read his mind, his dad said, "Now, Cody. You know that we don't keep secrets in this household. We're family. We don't hide from each other."

After Cody still didn't respond, his dad added with a bit of humor, "Plus, I'll always find you under your blanket anyway!"

With this, he got another small laugh from Cody.

In his gentle way, his dad launched into a story. "You know, when I was your age, we had a cat named Kibby. He used to lie around all day staring out the windows and watching the squirrels and other animals run around outside. I felt really bad, like maybe he was sad or something. So you know what I did?"

Cody looked up at his father, trying not to show how intrigued he was.

"I opened the screen door, and I told Kibby to run out and never come back. And do you know what he did? He lay right there. Never moving, just letting the breeze through his fur. You see, Cody, some animals are meant for the outside and the forest, like eagles and bears, but some animals are made for the inside. So, I need you to tell me, son, did you let the parakeets out this morning?"

The only sound now was the Legos rattling around in Cody's hands as he stared down at the floor, hiding his face from his dad.

Almost quiet enough not to be heard, Cody muttered, "I just wanted them to be free. They looked so sad in that cage all day long, you know? I thought maybe they wanted to fly around like the other birds get to."

Cody's dad went down onto the floor to look up into his son's eyes. "Cody, buddy. The birds are inside birds, not outside birds. They've been inside their whole lives; they don't know how to be outside birds. They probably won't survive the night. They don't know how to get food or where to go for shelter because we always provided that. Do you understand?"

Immediately, his eyes began to well up with the awareness of what he may have just done. "So, because I let them out...I killed them?" Tears ran down his cheeks, and he tried to apologize.

"I didn't mean to...to...kill..." He broke into tears, unable to get the words out any longer.

"I know, son. That cage was the only thing keeping them alive. Sometimes it's the things we feel are trapping us that are actually helping us in life. Those birds needed their cage."

"Can we go out and find them then? Bring them back inside?" Cody asked with a slight sense of hope in his voice.

"I know you want to, but it's probably too late, buddy. They've probably already begun to explore the forest. There's no way to know for sure where they went. But look at it like this: I'm sure the birds are happy to have some freedom for the time being."

Cody twiddled his thumbs, still looking at the floor. Slowly, he started to gather himself and asked, "Dad, can I be alone for a little bit?"

"Sure, son. But remember, you can't be too hard on yourself. Know that you were trying to help, but there's more to a story than what we think is best for someone else. Only when we get the full picture can we do the right thing. Those birds had a good life."

With that, his dad slowly walked out of his room, leaving Cody alone with his thoughts.

A sense of determination began to form inside Cody. He grabbed his drawing book and colored pencils and set to drawing his best image of the two birds that had been alive and well in their cage just this morning.

After finishing his drawing, Cody ran downstairs and propped it up in the birdcage, right where the parakeets used to sing their songs. As if making a vow, Cody muttered, "Don't worry. I'll find you. I promise."

Cody looked at both of his parents with remorse in his eyes and said, "Mom, Dad, is it alright if I spend the night up in the treehouse? If they hear me out there, maybe they'll come to me and be safe up there."

His parents looked at each other. His dad only shrugged. His mom, with a bit of frustration toward his dad, replied, "Please just be careful up there. Remember that you have the radio if you need anything at all from us. Take your dinner, and I'll come get the dishes in a bit."

A smile formed on his face. Cody grabbed his plate of spaghetti, then sprinted out the door, leaving it wide open behind him, and started to scramble up the ladder to his safe haven.

Back in the kitchen, Nicole confronted Rex.

"What in the world did you say to him? It looked like he'd seen a ghost."

Rex considered the thought and said, "The truth, I guess. He needed to hear it. It's hard to see our boy hurt like that, but it's only for the best."

Nicole stared silently out the window before she responded. "I guess you're right. The truth is hard, but he can't live in a shadow for his entire life. Just know, if he calls tonight, you're the one who has to go out and check on him."

She walked away towards the couch and paused to shout back, "And you're cleaning the dishes!"

Up in the treehouse, Cody sprinkled birdseed along the windowsill and then propped a flashlight against the shutter to light the way.

As he tucked himself under the blanket to dig into the plate of noodles, his only thoughts were about the parakeets. Where were they now? Were they okay? Did he put out enough birdseed?

Before he could take his last bite, he slumped backward and gave in to the exhaustion of a long day.

CHAPTER TWO

Cody takes the stairs by twos to go out searching for the birds he'd set free.

It's been a long and difficult search, but Cody still hasn't given up hope. There's a part of him that can almost feel those birds out there, soaring through the sky and looking for him to bring them home.

Every day he hops on his bike and rides for hours looking for those birds. Today, he's going out to check around the lake just west of the family's cabin. It's part of his plan. He'll slowly cover the entire area until he finds those birds and brings them home safely.

He walks out the front door, where the two parakeets lay, side by side, illuminated by a ray of sunshine as if set there to display Cody's biggest mistake.

Immediately, Cody is on his knees with his face buried in his hands, sobbing. He tries to stand up and run away, but the parakeets always seem to follow him, telling him over and over about the mistake he's made.

Covered in sweat, Cody ripped the covers off his face; having thrashed around throughout his nightmare, he almost ripped the sheets off the bed entirely. This was the third time in the last six months he'd had the exact same dream.

He had found the parakeets dead at the foot of the tree fort only a few days after he released them, but that experience had become a recurring dream. It was starting to weigh heavily on him, affecting how much he wanted to get out and ride his bike in the same forest those birds had tried to be free in.

Voices downstairs reminded him of the big day he had ahead of him, so he rushed to get dressed and splashed some water on his face to forget the night of sleep he just had.

In the kitchen was Ryan. Ryan and Cody had been in school together since neither of them could form full sentences, let alone crack jokes with one another the way they did now. Ryan was similarly built, without the massively long legs that made up Cody's lower half. They both had the same dirty blond hair that always looked even dirtier from the amount of time they spent outside and bright green eyes that allowed them to get away with almost anything in school.

Cody and Ryan took pride in the fact that their teachers often confused the two of them when they were sitting down. Once they stood up and Cody towered over everyone, the teachers would make their apologies and awkwardly shuffle away.

The two boys could never control their laughter in these moments.

Every week the boys schemed for the weekend. They looked at trail maps, spoke with local rangers, and begged their parents for permission before heading out and getting on their mountain bikes. It was what they lived for.

"Ryan! I stayed up all night teaching myself about topographic maps! You'll never believe what I found."

Cody's mom had learned to expect what came next, so she rushed to clear the table of the plates left over from her and Rex's rushed breakfast.

Slamming a map down on the table and unfolding it, Cody started drawing lines this way and that, as if anyone could understand what he meant.

Ryan grabbed Cody's shoulders to steady him. "Hey! Take a chill pill, man! I want to understand what's going on here. What's a...top-graph?"

"Topographic! It shows you how steep the hills are. Imagine how strong we can get on our bikes if we plan routes with huge hills!"

The confusion on Ryan's face slowly started to turn into excitement. It was always this way. Cody devoted every waking moment to mountain biking and figuring out how he could get better. Ryan just loved riding with him.

"So check it out. This trail goes up over a thousand feet before we take the backside down to cross the river. I bet right now it's starting to get snow, which will make it super fun to ride."

"Snow? Already? I thought we were biking, not skiing." Ryan always complained about the cold, but Cody couldn't be stopped.

"Yeh, snow! It'll give us something to work our turns on. I saw this great video of a guy up in Alaska riding his bike all over the snow. Plus, when he fell, it was right into the snow, and there's no way it hurt."

At the first hint of crashing bikes, Cody's mom jumped in.

"Boys! Everyone take a breather. It's nine in the morning, for Pete's sake. I'm not letting you go out there until we've sat down and talked about your safety plans."

"Mom! I'm not stupid!"

"Nor did I say you were. It's about to be hibernation season, and the bears out there are getting ready to lay low for the winter. That means getting fat. By whatever means necessary. And I won't let you two boys become dinner for a bear just because you're making rash decisions."

Cody couldn't even stand still. He fidgeted with the map and packed it into his bag with a little compass his dad had gotten him last Christmas.

"Alright, alright, give us your speech so we can go already."

"Thank you." She grabbed two fresh plates of pancakes and set them in front of the two boys, pulling her hands back quickly as if they were in danger of becoming breakfast as well. The boys immediately began feasting.

It was the move every mom with young boys knew. Put food in their mouths, and they won't be able to argue back.

"First, you're taking bear spray. You know where it is in the garage, so grab two cans and put them in your bike bags. Second, you *will* be home by dinner time. If you're not, your father will be out there looking for you and unhappy to be doing it."

Cody tried to protest through a mouthful of pancakes, but only a brief and muffled "Moooom" got out.

Cody's mom continued on with no regard for Cody's pancake-corked words. "Finally, if you see a bear you...do what?"

"Stand your ground, make yourself big, and get your spray ready," both of the boys simultaneously responded through their final bites as if they had recited this a million times before.

"Exactly. And you know where the ranger station is, so you head straight there and call us immediately. You don't go past the Outpost ranger station; it's too far from home. Your dad's ranger buddies will tell us if you fly through there, so no tricks!"

When his mom didn't continue any further, Cody turned to Ryan, and without a word, both boys stood up and made for the door.

****

The trails were lightly frosted with fresh snow, but it didn't slow Cody and Ryan down a bit. The boys sped through the forest with an intimate knowledge of the twists and turns of the trail system. They'd been here a million times before and had made this their second home.

Ryan was significantly slower than Cody Long Legs, no matter how hard he tried to keep up. In a mixture of competition and young foolishness, Ryan pedaled up toward Cody and gave him a light shoulder tap.

The grin across Cody's face grew in a way that told Ryan he had made a huge mistake.

Cody quickly slammed the front brake on and made an aggressive maneuver down a steep single-track trail they rarely ever attempted. Behind him, he could hear Ryan struggling to turn around and follow.

Thinking it would be funny to see the look on Ryan's face, Cody stopped halfway down the hill and waited for him to come around the sharp bend. His plan was to only spook him a bit, but Ryan was jumpy and nowhere near as good of a rider as Cody.

When Ryan came cruising around the bend, Cody growled as if a bear were hiding right beside the trail. It was enough to startle Ryan and send him just off the trail.

The crash itself probably should have done more damage than it did.

Cody ran to Ryan in a mixture of concern and laughter. Once he saw Ryan grinning from underneath his helmet, he burst out laughing.

The two of them shared moments like this often. The competition turned fierce, and the playful banter typically ended with one of them off their bike.

"Dude. I thought you were a big mama bear about to swipe my head right off."

"You should have seen it. I thought you were toast once you went off the trail!"

Both of the boys fell back, tired from laughing so hard and biking all day long. The silence of the forest took over. It did a fair amount of the speaking in this friendship, always coming up at the right moments.

And then something interrupted the silence. A single snap of a twig, followed by rustling leaves just loud enough to spark concern.

In a panic, Cody grabbed for his bag to get his hands on the bear spray, expecting to see a massive bear looming over them.

Instead, a small cub poked its head out of the bush. The big brown eyes and tiny muzzle were enough to immediately turn the fear into compassion and care.

The forest creatures had always been Cody's soft spot. "Do you think it's alone? Its mom could have lost it, right?"

"Mama bears never leave their cubs alone. We've got to get out of here." Ryan's fear was starting to break through the cool demeanor he would often put on.

"Well, I'm not leaving him here! Look, let's get up in this tree and wait to see if the mom is around. Let's go!"

There was a nearby pine tree that still had branches low enough for the two boys to use to climb up. After resting their bikes against the trunk, Cody took the initiative and started straight up.

Twenty feet off the ground, they stopped and got comfortable. Next to mountain biking, climbing trees was key to this friendship. One boy would always push the other to go higher and higher until both of them were secretly scared and started coming up with excuses to get back down.

Cody pulled some extra layers out of his backpack and tossed them over to Ryan. "I don't think we'll need to be here too long. The mom never goes far. But just in case, let's at least stay warm."

Pulling on a wool sweater that Cody's aunt had made, Ryan could only start to laugh again. "This is like one of those Hardy Boys books we read last year! But instead, we're like...bear detectives!"

"Exactly! And I'm not going home until we solve this mystery."

"Didn't Mr. Gloucester say in science that some mama bears will abandon their cubs if they don't think they'll survive the winter?"

"Mr. Gloucester's boring. I can't ever stay awake in his classes. But maybe he was right."

"So what if she's not coming? This cub's going to die. It's freezing out here."

Cody looked around a bit more, thinking over all of his options. "Well, if the mom doesn't come back for the cub in the next hour, we'll take it home and figure out how to explain it to my parents on the way."

"Cody, are you sure about this? I mean, it's a bear, not a puppy. You can't just let it curl up at the foot of your bed all winter."

"The only thing I'm sure of is that this bear doesn't deserve to die out here. So I won't let it."

After an hour of swinging their legs to try and stay warm, Cody finally made the call. "I think we can head down. That cub looks like it's freezing, and we haven't heard a peep."

"Yeh, let's get going. I can barely feel my toes anyway." Ryan started climbing down the tree towards the cub.

As Cody followed him down, he started hashing out his plan. "I think if we get the cub wrapped up in that sweater you're wearing, we can put it in my backpack with the zipper just barely closed. That way, the bear can still look around and enjoy the ride as much as I do!"

"Great! Now just come up with some magic plan to convince your mom and dad not to lock you in your room so you'll never see your bike for the rest of eternity."

"Don't worry about that. My dad's a total softy."

✳✳✳✳

From the tree line, Cody could make out the silhouettes of his parents in the fading daylight. Even from there, part of him knew that he was about to be in trouble.

He'd thought about his plan the entire ride home, but he still had no idea what to tell his parents about the little bear cub riding along in his backpack. He was worried, but the warmth of the bear's nose on his neck the entire way home had only strengthened his resolve and desire to save this bear.

Cody and Ryan's bikes rolled up, and both of Cody's parents were silent. Never a good sign.

"Mom, Dad, just hear me out."

His parents just stood there. Staring. Until a ruffle came from the backpack and Cody's mom's jaw hit the floor.

"CODY?? Ryan?? WHAT IS THAT? Tell me that is NOT a bear in your backpack!"

She began to pace frantically, eventually stopping right in front of her husband.

"Rex. What in the HELL is going on here?"

"Okay, Nicole. Calm down." Turning to Cody, Rex attempted to compose himself. "Cody. Take the backpack off and set it on the ground. Once it's there, we can talk about this. Ryan, I suggest you head home now, son."

As if he was waiting for the excuse, Ryan turned to go. "Yes, sir. I'll see you all tomorrow." From behind him, he could hear Cody begin the long discussion with his parents.

"I swear he's friendly! He rode on my back this entire way! His mom abandoned him–"

"Cody. As I said, put the bag down. I won't ask again."

Slowly, Cody pulled the bag from his shoulders and gently placed it on the ground next to him. The bear only laid its head down and began to softly snore, earning a small pique in interest from Cody's mom.

"See, it's so nice! We can take care of him and help him get better until the spring! I'll do all the work, clean up after him, feed him, anything!"

Cody's dad let out a low chuckle that broke the tension completely.

"Son, we don't know anything about raising a bear cub. It needs its mother to survive. How do you suppose we turn ourselves into big black bears to hibernate up against all winter?"

"Can't we call Doc Murphy? He's a great vet! He saved the Ashbys' goats last summer, you remember?"

"I suppose we'll have to now. Nicole, would you go grab that old dog crate we still have lying around in the basement? I think it's just underneath the stack of National Geographics down there."

Cody's mom went off to the basement, still looking hesitant about the whole situation. But her husband, the park ranger, would be able to figure this out, so she put her trust in him entirely.

While she was off searching for the dog crate, Rex sent Cody to put away his bike and clean himself up. He grabbed his phone and called up Dr. Murphy, the county vet.

Laughing to himself, Rex stood in the driveway, attempting to explain the situation to the disbelieving veterinarian on the other end of the line. After a while of trying to convince him this was more than just entertaining a young boy, Dr. Murphy agreed to come over.

All Rex could do was sit and stare at the bear as it slept soundly in his son's backpack.

Before Cody was born, Rex had worked countless overnight shifts at the Ranger station. The Forest Service had been struggling to get workers at the time, and Rex loved being there, so he would apologize to Nicole or sometimes bring her along with him.

That particular night, Nicole had been off visiting her parents, and Rex had snatched up a whole week's worth of overtime hours. They had a baby due in less than four months, and the extra cash would be a lifesaver.

Each time Rex worked the night shift, he would start the evening with a walk through the forest to some of his favorite spots. He passed by the fields of daisies and daffodils that bloomed in the springtime, the overlook that made him feel small as the river rushed around bends hundreds of feet below him, and finally, the old homestead that the park kept intact for visitors to check out.

By the time he had reached the homestead that evening, dusk had just started to settle in, and the world was beginning to prepare for sleep.

But Rex got a sense that his night had just begun.

He heard a rustling from behind the cabin as if something was distressed.

Since he was a kid, Rex had always had a massive soft spot for animals. He brought dogs home off the streets and begged his mom and dad to keep them. Once, he managed to hide a puppy in his room for a week before his parents even noticed the extra lunch meat disappearing from the fridge at a worrying rate.

So when he saw the deer stuck in the wire fence behind the homestead, his heart ached.

As a Ranger, they teach you that it's always best to let nature take its course. It was the one part of being a Ranger that Rex disagreed with, and he always put the animals first, not the Forest Service.

He carefully approached the buck with a stunning six-point rack crowned on its head. Its antlers had managed to get tangled up in the fence, a predicament that had only gotten worse with all the thrashing it was doing.

"Hey there, buddy. It's just me. I'm not going to hurt you," Rex voiced calmly, letting the buck know he was there.

"If you let me, I'm going to try and get you out of here. But I need your help, and you'll have to stay still. Otherwise, I might accidentally hurt you."

A lot of the other Rangers teased Rex about his soft spot for animals.

He knew that he would get flack for it, that they would have told him he should have brought venison home for dinner, but he never let their teasing get in the way of doing what felt right.

From the corner of his eye, Rex noticed a small doe approaching. He was startled at first but calmed his body and spoke softly to the doe.

"Hi there, beautiful. You must be this guy's little lovebird, aren't you?"

The doe just stared directly back at him, making no move.

"Alright, you just hang out right there and I'll try to get to work here."

Rex pulled out his multi-tool while still calmly talking to both the buck and the doe. At this point, the buck had stopped its incessant fighting with the fence, so Rex was able to get a decent vantage point and start snipping wires away.

At the first cut of a wire, the buck thrashed and tried to break free. Its whole body slammed against Rex, knocking him backward and onto the ground.

"Whoa there, buddy. It's alright. You're not free just yet, so you'll have to let me work," he said to the buck as he slowly got back on his feet.

Unfazed, Rex continued hacking away at the fence, the doe right there by his side.

After about half an hour of working with his small set of wire cutters, the buck was just about free.

He clipped the final few wires and told the buck that it was free to go be with its partner now.

The buck pulled back, free from the fence, and stared into Rex's eyes. For what felt like an eternity, the two of them were locked on each other before the buck broke contact, brushed its nose against Rex's shoulder, and ran to the doe before bounding off into the forest.

Rex chuckled to himself and wiped the beading sweat from his brow.

The last of the daylight was just falling behind the trees, and Rex knew that he should get back before full nightfall. When he stood up, he could tell that the fence was only a danger to other wildlife at this point.

Without hesitation, he pulled out a lantern, strapped on a headlamp, and got to work tearing the whole fence down. It had no purpose other than decoration, and Rex didn't want to see any other deer snared by this useless fence. He spent hours that night tearing the fence down, alone in the dark.

The next day, he told no one about what had happened. He kept that little moment between him and the two deer to himself until the day he told five-year-old Cody the story.

What he didn't tell Cody was how he still saw those two deer to this day. They always stopped and shared a silent and still moment with Rex whenever he was out on the trail. Then they all went their separate ways until their next encounter.

Looking at the little cub that Cody had just brought home, Rex wondered if Cody would ever get to experience something like that – – or had he just made a huge mistake letting him keep that bear?

CHAPTER THREE

The dust from his old Jeep Wrangler was visible before the car itself, but they all knew that Doc Murphy was blasting up their driveway to see what trouble Cody had gotten himself into this time.

Like clockwork, Cody came sprinting through the front door with his head still dripping water from the failed attempts to scrub the dirt from his face. He figured he would deal with the fallout later, but he couldn't miss this.

"Dad! Is that Doc Murphy? He agreed to come out then?"

Cody's dad had moved the small cub into the dog crate that used to house their old Labrador before Rex and Nicole even had Cody.

He finished folding an old blanket and stashed it in the corner for the bear to cozy up in. "Yeh, I suppose that is. Didn't think he'd be here for another hour or so, but he must be intrigued. Can't blame him."

When the doc rolled up, he went straight toward the bear without saying a word. For a few minutes, he checked its vital signs and finally turned to the McCully family with a confused look on his face.

"So, you found it? Just sitting there in the snow?"

Cody couldn't hold back and immediately launched into the entire story. Even in the excitement, he didn't forget to include details about how much faster he was riding than Ryan was.

Doc Murphy just shook his head. "Whoa there, sonny. Slow yourself down. Where'd you find her exactly?"

"Her?! It's a girl? Dang, I was so sure it was a boy. Uh, yeh, I guess we found her out on Phantom Spur Trail, maybe like three miles from the trailhead."

"Well, you might want to stay away from there for a bit. Could be that there's a pretty angry mama bear out there looking for her cub. Most likely, she left her behind. This one's not in the best shape."

"How do we save her then? I can make the basement into a den! I'll bring sticks and pine boughs and really build it up like the mom might have done. Do you think she'll drink milk? Would she drink out of a bottle? How much?"

The questions went on like that for a minute before Rex turned to Cody to calm him down. "Listen up, Cody. I know you're excited. There's a lot we need to do if she's going to make it through the winter. Let's hear the Doc out before jumping to any conclusions."

"Thanks, Rex. Didn't know how to cut that excitement off without feeling bad. Yes, Cody. She'll drink milk. And a lot of it, I presume. She's pretty skinny, so she needs to be fattened up before you tuck her away for the winter."

Cody's dad interrupted again just as Cody began to shoot off on another tangent of questions. "Doc, can we take a minute to go inside and talk just the two of us? Nicole, you and Cody should head to the store. It sounds like we may need some milk."

Nicole pulled the car keys out of her pocket and started guiding Cody toward the car. "Way ahead of ya! We'll be back in, say, thirty minutes?"

"Perfect. See you then."

Although it was obvious Cody wanted to fight his parents on this one, he hopped into the car and went with his mom to the store down the road, unable to let his mind think about anything but keeping this bear alive through the winter.

Back at the house, Rex and Doc Murphy sat down over a cup of tea and discussed what it would really look like to have a bear in the house.

"Look, I'm not gonna sugar-coat it for you, Rex. It's not going to be easy. She might not live through the winter. It's why the mom left her out to die in the first place."

"You must not know Cody too well. Other than riding that bike of his, all he does is care about animals, especially when they're that young and small."

"Yeh, I remember that. You told me about the parakeets this summer. He's a real animal lover, that one."

"So, if we set up the basement and get a space heater down there, you think it'll be enough?"

"I think that's about all you really can do," the doc said. "Feed it about three times a day. It probably won't sleep through the winter, so Cody's gonna have to feed it constantly."

The corner of Rex's mouth twitched up and stayed there. "Cody won't miss a beat caring for that cub. I guarantee it."

Rex grabbed the empty mugs off the table and tossed them in the sink. "Thanks for coming over, Doc. I'd love to sit and catch up, but I think I've got a bit of work to do. I haven't been down in that basement for years."

As Doc Murphy drove away from the house, Rex headed around back to the basement door. He'd taken the space heater out of his own home office to try to create the most realistic den possible.

By the time Cody and his mom got home, Rex had completely transformed the basement. He had moved some boxes and crates to create a mini bear cave. The bear cub had been placed inside a dog cage and was already fast asleep.

He'd already heated up the milk they had left and put it into one of Cody's old baby bottles. The excitement to try and feed the cub was obvious on Cody's face, and all Rex needed to do was hand it to him.

"Be careful now. You'll want to take it slow. She may not know what's going on."

Cody took the cub in his arms, gently woke her up, and introduced the bottle to her lips. It took no time at all. The cub grabbed right on and started drinking milk as if her life depended on it.

The grin on Cody's face could have brought enough warmth to that basement, space heater or not.

The winter that followed wasn't an easy one. Headlines consistently showed record-breaking snowfalls and temperatures dropping far below the national average.

Even amidst the blizzards and freezing temperatures, Cody never missed a beat. He spent more time in the basement with that cub during that winter than he did anywhere else. His tree fort sat empty. Rex and Nicole often found him down there in the middle of the night or early in the morning before school.

He put his all into it.

The cub grew and grew. At the beginning of the winter, she weighed just under 5 pounds. In February, Cody weighed her every day, and she was consistently hitting over 20 pounds. By March, she was 30 pounds.

Doc Murphy made regular visits to the McCully house that winter. Every time he came, there was only good news that came with him.

When spring started to show up, Cody's mom and dad sat him down to talk about what needed to happen next.

The level of maturity that Cody handled the situation with surprised both of his parents.

"Okay. So this must be when we come up with the plan to get her back out there?"

Cody's parents looked at each other. It was his mom that could talk first.

"Yes, Cody. She needs to be back out in her natural habitat. She can't go on living in the basement like that." She paused before adding, "I really hope you know how proud I am of the love you've given this cub."

"Thanks mom." Cody then looked at his dad, "Dad, I've organized a plan with Ryan on how to take her back to the same spot. Hopefully, her mom will show up and take her back in. What do you think?"

"I think that's a great idea, but we're doing this as a team, end of discussion."

Cody hesitated briefly. "Alright. I'll talk to Ryan. Can we go out tomorrow to take her back? I think it's supposed to be a nice day. She'll like that, you know?"

"Yes, she will. Go hit the hay; we'll get her loaded up tomorrow morning." Rex gave Cody a tight squeeze and a kiss on his forehead before pushing him up toward his bedroom as he reluctantly looked backward.

The next day, Cody was up before the sun. He strapped on his already-prepared backpack with the baby bear inside and headed outside to wait for his dad.

As he stood there fussing with his backpack, trying to get the baby bear comfortable, his dad came out, steaming cup of coffee in hand.

"Mornin', buddy. I see you don't want to waste any time today."

"Hey, Dad. Yeh, can we go out early so we can find a good spot to set up and stay out a while. We want to watch the grand reunion."

"Well, listen up real quick. Work just called, and I've got to go in for the morning. So I think that's going to mean we have to wait a day or two to get her back out there. I'm really sorry, but we'll get her home safely."

"What?! Dad! That's not fair at all! But we're ready!"

Rex moved toward his old truck in a rush to get to work. "I'm really sorry, Cody! We'll take her out tomorrow, I promise."

He got in his truck and drove off toward the park.

Through his dust cloud, Ryan rode up. He had arranged to meet Cody bright and early and could already see the sadness on Cody's face.

"Hey, Cody! What's up?"

"My dad had to go to work. So he can't take us out today like he promised."

"Well, I guess we could just go on a ride? Maybe the cub wants a few more days here anyway."

"No! Today's the day. Listen. My mom's still asleep. We can easily get out there before she gets up and probably be back before she starts to freak out too much."

Before Ryan even had the chance to respond, Cody had jumped on his bike and was pedaling away from the house.

The boys rode off toward the trails linking the McCully cabin and the National Forest. They had a lot of riding to do today, but those boys had ridden this exact trail so many times before that they didn't think twice about it.

By the time the boys got to where they had determined earlier as the right spot to drop the cub, the sun was directly overhead. They'd ridden for nearly four hours, and both of them were exhausted.

Cody got off his bike first, carried his backpack over to the clearing in the forest, and took out the cub. "Alright, I think that if we leave her here, we might be able to have a good vantage point from that big pine over there."

Ryan nodded in agreement. "Don't you think we should, I don't know, roll the cub around a bit and get our smell off her?"

"Good idea. Here, you do the same thing. We don't want the mom to smell us either." Cody was down on the ground, rolling around like it was a first-grade fire drill before Ryan could register what he had even said.

"Oh. Okay," Ryan said hesitantly as he slowly lowered himself to the ground, following Cody's lead.

Cody hopped up and started rubbing dirt all over the cub.

"Alright! That should do it. Let's go stash our bikes and get up in the tree. I imagine that the bear will come around at some point."

The baby cub started making some low whining noises as if calling out to Cody and Ryan to come back. Both of the boys stopped and looked toward the cub before heading off with the hope that the mama bear would hear the distress calls and come running.

Ryan led the charge upwards, with Cody following. As they made their way higher, they heard some noises coming through the brush behind them.

The noises quickened their pace along with their heart rates, and they sped skyward to the highest branches they could reach. As soon as they felt safe higher up, the boys risked a glance backward.

What they saw was astonishing. Another cub had wandered toward the one Cody had given all of his spare time this past winter to. It was easy, like two kids meeting on the playground.

The two cubs were immediately enthralled with each other. They were rolling, play-fighting, nipping at each other, and acting as if they'd been friends forever.

Cody didn't know if the mother would show up any time soon or not, and the sun was already starting to go down. He needed a plan that would get the mother there sooner rather than later.

His answer was, of course, reliant upon his bike.

"Alright, Ryan. Here's my plan. I think we should both hop on our bikes and circle the area. The mom is bound to be here somewhere, and we can probably attract her just by making some noise riding around. Then, whoever she finds first will lead her right back here. It'll work; I know it."

"I dunno, Cody. That sounds pretty sketchy. I'm pretty sure black bears run up to like thirty miles per hour."

"That's nothin'. Let's go!"

With hesitation, Ryan started to climb down the tree with Cody, and the boys mounted their bikes.

Cody was off first, powering up the steep hill with the ease that his long legs had always given him.

Ryan went the other direction, hoping to keep to flat ground.

After a few minutes of riding around, Ryan heard Cody shout in the distance.

"Ryan! I'VE GOT HER! I'M COMING IN HOT!"

Ryan barely had time to turn around to see Cody fly past him at an ungodly speed down the steep hill back toward where the cubs were still playing. Only a few seconds later, a massive black bear came bounding down the hill after him.

When Cody got to the clearing where the two cubs were playing, he slammed on the brakes and ditched his bike to run up in the tree as the mother came right behind him.

As soon as the mother saw her cub with another, she changed directions and bolted toward her own. She stopped just short of the two cubs, neither of which even looked her way.

Ryan made his way around the back of the clearing to slowly sneak up into the tree. He sat beside Cody to wait and see what would happen.

All of a sudden, the mama bear reared up on both legs and came down quickly toward the cub that was new to her.

As her arm swept backward, winding up to deliver a devastating blow, her own cub stepped in the way.

The mother's arm stopped instantly. Her own cub stood its ground, protecting its newfound friend, who was now cowering behind it.

Cody and Ryan watched with amazement and curiosity as to what could possibly happen next. Thoughts raced through Cody's head, but he had no idea what to do.

Ultimately, the two boys didn't make a move. It was clear that the bears needed to sort this out between them, and their interference would only damage the natural interaction that was taking place right before them.

The moment seemed to hang suspended in time, never to move forward or resolve the situation.

When it finally happened, Ryan had forgotten to breathe, and Cody was there, shaking him back into reality.

"Ryan! Come on, look what's happening!"

The cub that Cody had grown to love so deeply slowly made her way around to the mother bear. As the towering mother came back down to all fours, her own cub stayed close to Cody's, continuing to provide its protection.

The mother slowly moved her snout toward Cody's cub and sniffed. She gave her a long inspection from snout to tail without any signs of what she was thinking.

The mother's own cub walked up to her and nudged her with her nose as if telling her that they should move on.

At this moment, Cody wasn't sure what exactly was going to happen. He began to think about all of the ways he could keep his cub alive forever at home, maybe train her like he would a dog. But he knew that this wasn't truly possible.

Right when he was beginning to feel the failure of finding the mother but having his cub be rejected, the mother reached out and took Cody's cub by the scruff of her neck. The small trio of bears then turned and strolled back into the bushes, leaving no trace of their presence other than a flattened patch of grass and two young boys, one of whom had started to let tears of joy come rolling down his cheeks.

"Cody! We've got to go, man. The sun is already going down, and I don't know how much time my headlamp battery has left in it. My mom is probably freaking out."

Cody shook himself back into the present. "Oh, shoot. Yeh. Let's ride!"

The boys went back down the tree to grab their bags and their bikes. They rode back down toward the McCully cabin through the fading light that just barely made its way through the dense canopy.

"Dude. Did you see yourself back there? You must have been going at least forty miles per hour."

"Huh? You really think so? I dunno. I was just so scared. That bear was about to bite my butt right off."

"It was insane. We have to go to the bike park and see just how fast you can get going. All you need to do is pretend you're being chased by another bear."

Cody was lost in his own head. There was a mix of complete joy over getting the cub home, worry about coming home so late, and overall exhaustion from the long day behind them.

"Ha. Yeh, I'll just become a pro bear chaser. That's it."

"I like that! Cody Long Legs, the Bear Chaser. You're gonna be famous one day. No one rides like you."

"Maybe. Let's just get home. I bet my dad's about to call all his ranger friends to go out searching for us. Come on, we'll take the shortcut."

He veered his bike sharply to the left down the single-track trail that he often tended to, trimming back the ivy that constantly tried to overtake the path. Cody knew he might be in trouble for not waiting for his dad to go with them, but he couldn't wait to tell them about what had just happened.

CHAPTER FOUR

The night came down without any warning with a frost that turned the roads slick and dangerous.

So far, this spring had seen average temperatures, with everyone thinking the final frost had already come and gone. The cold snap that came in on the day of the boys' ride out into the woods was so unexpected that no one could have seen it coming.

Nicole hadn't realized that Cody and Ryan had taken the bear cub on their bike ride until the late afternoon, when she decided to go down to the basement to check on the cub. She immediately contacted Rex.

Not only was Rex furious about the boys returning the cub on their own, but he also knew how dangerous it was to be out this late in the cold that was coming through. He had no intention of letting Cody and Ryan get caught out there.

His old truck fishtailed around just about every bend, but there was nothing in his head that pointed him toward turning around. He needed to find his boy.

He had left home as soon as the sun started going down. The cold was only predicted to get worse as the night progressed.

Rex knew these roads better than anyone else could claim to, but that didn't change how every curve presented the danger of throwing him off into the trees.

His old truck was his best friend. He bought it almost twenty years ago, way before Cody had ever been a thought in his mind. Since then, he cared for it, did all the work himself, and never let anyone else behind the wheel.

The thing about doing everything yourself is that you lose the second set of eyes that could have seen what you missed, like a set of tires just beyond their years with a tread that didn't want to do much more than slide around.

He never even thought about his tires until he started sliding.

The truck fishtailed as soon as he hit the curve. Rex pulled to the right, trying to correct the truck's direction, but there was nothing more than ice for his bald tires to grab onto.

At forty miles per hour, there wasn't much hope for Rex and his polished forest green 1980 Ford Ranger. The car flew straight off the road, almost silently, with all the new snow to muffle the sound of the crash.

For a few moments, Rex felt like it was going to be okay. He didn't feel too badly hurt, just shocked. Then he realized where he was and how firmly the truck had him in its grip.

He wasn't too far off the road, but the steering wheel had warped in such a way that it had pinned him to his seat. He fought with every ounce of his power, but he was lodged beneath the wheel with no way out.

Each time Rex tried to move, he seemed to get himself even more stuck.

The only thing that was on his mind was his boy. Even when the truck's front end had wrapped itself around that massive pine, he only hoped that Cody was okay.

Once he realized that there was no fighting his way free, Rex simply gave in and decided to wait for help. He imagined that someone would be on their way from the Ranger station, or at least he hoped there would be.

His mind wandered back and forth to the memories of his own childhood and playing in the forest. He started to see how much of himself Cody had picked up.

In that moment, he only felt saddened, realizing that he might not get to see the man Cody would grow into.

He knew that if he wasn't able to escape that Nicole would be okay. He married her because of how strong she was, how independent she could be, and how amazing of a mother she would be. Rex only hoped she would forgive him for leaving the family so early on.

As the hours passed, Rex realized there wasn't much of a chance that anyone would be coming to his rescue. In this kind of a storm, no one would be going out. They would wait until morning to start the search.

The panic in him started to rise up again, and he started fighting against the steering wheel that had him trapped in place.

The surrounding storm seemed to only pick up as the night deepened. Lightning had been on the horizon all night, but now it had begun to make its way overhead.

Rex had been to this spot hundreds of times throughout his career. It was expected to go up in flames at any moment, as most of the trees had succumbed to beetles that were slowly destroying most of the spruces around the northwest.

He'd fought multiple small fires over the years that had been started by storms exactly like the one he looked up at now.

In a blinding flash of light, a monstrous crash sounded from nearby. A once towering spruce toppled, falling right behind Rex's truck.

After the lightning hit and the tree fell, the world felt still.

He shook himself back into the present and continued trying to unpin himself from the cage that his car had become.

The smell of smoke began to drift through the air. At first, it was only the smell of burning wood-- the same smell that Rex had fond memories of from lighting fires to heat the family cabin every winter.

Now, that smell started to turn into the scent of burning oil and chemicals that could only have come from his truck.

The smoke billowed from the bed of the truck straight into the cab, surrounding Rex with smoke.

He fought to hold his breath as he wrestled with the steering wheel, eventually needing to give in and take a full breath of the thick smoke that had filled the cab.

No matter what he did, the wheel wouldn't budge.

His lungs were filled with smoke, making him unable to continue breathing.

Rex's world went black.

It wasn't until three days later that Cody and Nicole heard anything about Rex. Three days filled with calling the rangers, Rex's old buddies, and begging for answers. Still, nothing.

Cody fought his mom day in and day out, insisting that he go out looking for his dad. After long exchanges and heated debates, he finally realized that if he hadn't ever gone out, his dad might not have gotten lost out there.

Rex's best friend and long-time coworker showed up at their door that afternoon.

"Nicole..."

She had barely gotten the door open before she fell to the floor. Her sobs and muffled screams were sent out into the trees surrounding their family cabin.

Back in the family room, Cody stood alone. Within seconds, he bolted past his mom and his dad's old friends, straight up to the treehouse he had once sat and watched his dad work on every day.

When Nicole was able to stand, the rangers brought her inside to try and talk with her. While they had known her for years, there was no person in this world that could deliver this news with ease.

"Just tell me what happened. I need to know where Rex is."

"Nicole...he's not coming back from this one."

She fell straight back into unintelligible sobs until she was finally able to ask, "Where was he? What happened? I can handle it."

"We found his truck. He'd probably gotten himself turned around on some roads that aren't meant to be open this time of year. It was way back in the snowbank, which is why it probably took us so long to find it."

"And...Rex?"

"Well, Nicole, he was there. Looks like the steering wheel pinned him in. Can't have been long before he was gone."

"I...I don't know what to do. What am I going to tell Cody? I can't be a single mother...oh, no, what am I going to do?"

The ranger took her in close, just like he'd seen Rex do over the years when Nicole got stressed about Cody's free-willed spirit.

She stayed there in the arms of an old friend, in the only comfort she could find.

Up in the treehouse, Cody was curled up on his old bean bag chair, looking out the window and hoping for an answer.

It took Cody's mom two days to get him out of the treehouse. She had spent the first night up there with him, refusing to leave his side for anything. The second night she gave him some space and only brought him his dinner after sitting with him throughout the day.

Nicole arranged all of the services, calling Rex's extended family and completing all of the must-do tasks that no one ever wants to do in these moments.

Over the next few days, Ryan visited constantly, and Nicole started to see Sally coming around more often.

Sally, a tiny brunette ball of energy, was only a few days older than Cody. She'd been in his homeroom class since he started school, but Nicole never saw her around the house.

She vividly remembered how Rex had always teased Cody about Sally. He poked fun at him the way that dads do. These small memories brought glimpses of a smile to Nicole's face in the days following Rex's passing.

It was comforting for her to know that Cody had his friends.

She picked a day when both Ryan and Sally were over to go up to the treehouse and talk to Cody. She wanted to discuss Rex's funeral plans with him but didn't know how he would take it, and he was always in his best moods when his friends visited.

When she climbed up the ladder to the trap door entrance, the three kids were sitting there in silence, watching the trees move in the wind through the window. Ryan was the first to notice that Nicole had come inside.

"Oh, hey there, Mrs. McCully."

"Ryan, you know I always want you to call me Nicole. Hi there, Sally. How are you?"

"Hi, Mrs. McCully! I'm okay. We were just talking to Cody about maybe going and riding our bikes around for a bit. Would that be okay?"

"Of course. Can I just talk with Cody really quickly before you head out?"

Both Ryan and Sally nodded and disappeared through the trap door and down to their bikes, stashed right up against the tree.

"Cody, we need to talk about tomorrow's services. I was wondering if you wanted to say a few words?"

Cody muttered something, but Nicole couldn't hear a word.

"Buddy, I know you're hurting. I'm hurting. We all miss him so much." She was barely able to get the words out before breaking down into tears and sitting down in the bean bag chair next to Cody.

He put his arm around her and buried his head in her sweater. "Mom. I love you so much. I would love to talk about Dad tomorrow."

The two of them sat in silence for a long minute before Nicole gathered herself. "Thank you. He would have liked that very much. Maybe we'll even get you dressed up and looking sharp for him, yeh?"

She pinched his cheek and teased him a bit about looking good for Sally like Rex would have done if he were there.

"Stop it, Mom! She probably won't even be there!" Cody's smile was the first sign of the melting ice and the return of the boy she knew and loved so dearly.

"Well then, you better get down there and ask her to come! Go ride your bike. You deserve some time in the trees. Your dad would love to watch you keep riding."

"Thanks, Mom! I love you!" Cody was down the trap door in a heartbeat, sliding down the ladder he had helped build with his dad in the first days of construction.

Nicole sat in the treehouse for a few more minutes, watching the kids ride their bikes down the path and into the trees.

When she got up, she felt lighter. Seeing Cody smile, even so briefly, was exactly what she needed that day because the next was going to be hard.

Cody had biked past the church probably a hundred times when riding over to Ryan's house, but he'd definitely never set foot inside it.

The walls were a mixture of old stone masonry and delicately crafted stained glass windows that sent colorful light all around. Even with the high ceilings and bright flood lights, Cody felt trapped.

There wasn't a single plant inside this place. Was this anything like what his dad would have wanted?

Just when he started to feel the anger bubbling up inside him, he felt someone, or two someones, grab onto both of his arms.

Ryan and Sally were there, smiling.

Cody couldn't help but smile as he let them guide him toward a seat in the front of the church where his mom was.

The funeral was by the books. There was a short service where a priest talked a lot about heaven, and then it was time for Cody to get up and talk about his dad.

He took one last glance to his right at Sally, took a deep breath, and got up. He slowly walked to the front of the church, finding his way toward the microphone in the giant building.

There was a small step stool that he climbed up onto so he could reach the podium.

The priest had laid out a few readings. He offered them to Cody for ideas of what to say, but Cody knew that he wasn't going to read anything. He simply nodded politely and said thank you.

His dad wouldn't want to hear anything other than Cody's own words.

"Um, hi, everyone," Cody started slowly. His nerves were growing now that he had made it to the front of the big crowd. It was huge. His dad had known so many people. Everyone loved him.

In the corner of his eye, he saw Ryan and Sally, both sitting there smiling big at him. Their goofy smiles made him actually start to laugh.

"My dad was awesome. You all knew that. He made me my treehouse. He made me laugh. He loved my mom so much. Sometimes he would dress up in his blue jeans and dance like Elvis."

That got a laugh from the crowded room.

"Anyway, I don't think I know what I'm supposed to say right now. But I love my dad. One day, I'm going to be just like him. But I'll be a better mountain biker. He wasn't very good at that. Thank you for coming today and for taking care of my mom."

Cody awkwardly got down from his step stool and returned to his seat in the front of the church. Sally reached over and grabbed his hand as soon as he got there.

The entire crowd that showed up that day could see the small crush and young romance start at this moment. Sally showed up for Cody that day, and even as an eleven-year-old, Cody knew how important that was.

After the funeral was over, Cody rode his bike back to his house with Ryan and Sally. The three of them changed out of their fancier attire and headed straight for the trees on their bikes.

Sally didn't ride her bike in the same way that Ryan and Cody did. She dragged behind, took turns slowly, and walked the steep uphill stretches. She was also the only person that Ryan had ever seen Cody wait up for.

Other than his friends, the time spent outside on the trails was the only thing that truly helped Cody.

In the coming weeks, Cody wouldn't see the inside of his house for more than the time it took him to get to his bed and back. Most nights he spent in the treehouse. It felt closer to his dad than anywhere in the house did.

Nicole got home a few hours later, exhausted from the hours of holding space for others while trying to grieve herself. She came inside, ordered a pizza to be delivered, and was asleep on the couch as soon as she hung up.

By the time Cody and his friends got home, the sun had set. There was a pizza on the front doorstep, surrounded by all the flowers that had been sent to their home.

The three of them sat on the front porch and devoured the cold pizza in a few minutes.

When the two others left for their own homes, Cody stayed on the porch. When Nicole woke up, she found him there. She wrapped him in a blanket, tucked a pillow under his head, and let him sleep.

The warmer spring weather was making its way in. The ice that had made Rex's truck slide off the road just two weeks before was completely gone.

These days passed slowly for Cody and his mom. Nicole struggled to keep the cabin afloat, and Cody would hardly come inside. The times that she did see him inside were only because he needed to fuel up before going back out onto his bike.

Every ounce of Cody's grief was poured into his riding. Even when he didn't have school, he was gone from sunrise to sunset on the trails behind their cabin.

As Cody got older, he found mountain biking competitions to enter, always encouraging Ryan to join him.

By fifteen, Cody was winning the divisions filled with 21-year-olds. There wasn't a single rider out there that could keep up with him. Ryan tried, but he always came in right behind him, taking second place at a large percentage of the races.

Cody was 18 when he got his first sponsorship. Ka-Pow energy drinks were throwing their label all over his bike and his clothes, even trying to get his mom to put their logo on her car.

The mountain biking industry was on fire with news of Cody Long Legs, the Bear Chaser.

His one small-time sponsorship turned into two, and it wasn't long until Cody had big-time sports labels approaching him, asking him to ride for them.

He was the youngest rider to take such a large number of downhill racing medals home with him. The magazines talked about him being fearless, riding like he had nothing to lose.

Every interview that Cody took on was focused on his dad. He always attributed his riding success to Rex. He was the one that had gotten him outside as a kid. He had bought him his first old beat-up Huffy. Without his dad, he never would have gotten where he was today.

And, of course, Sally. They had been inseparable ever since his father's funeral. She had chosen a university close to home so they could stick together. Cody stayed at the local community college.

By this point, school seemed like an afterthought. Cody sought out a summer internship with the National Park Service, following in his father's footsteps as he had always known he would do.

Cody's life was everything he wanted. His best friend and his girlfriend were at his side through everything. His mom was finally starting to put herself back out there, happy to be dating again.

It was the moments like these that Cody looked back on and wondered how he ever had it so good. He thought back on these moments when he wanted to remember what it was like to have the perfect life.

CHAPTER FIVE

The whir of the saw came howling out of the garage's open door as Sally opened the door to walk toward her husband.

"Hello! Anyone in there?"

Cody looked around, a bit confused. He flipped the protective face shield up to rest on his head.

He was wearing the same pair of overalls he did all his car work in and a simple white tee, less white than it once was. In his hands he had a Sawzall, stuck halfway into the top of an old, rust-orange Cadillac.

The roof was almost halfway off, but Cody was getting close to finishing his little project. He'd looked for a car like this for almost two years. To remove the roof without damaging all of the other electrical components, it needed to be the right car with the right design.

Eventually, it was Ryan that actually saw the Cadillac for sale a couple of towns over. Cody had gone the same day he heard about it and brought it directly home.

This wasn't the first time Cody, with the help of Ryan, had removed the car roof of a Cadillac. Back in high school, Cody had found a Cadillac just like this one. From the first day he could drive, Cody knew he needed the type of car that would let him feel the open air and see his surroundings.

He spent several summers searching for something that made him feel that way after his dad died, but now that he was driving, the stakes seemed even higher.

Without even asking his mom, Cody had shown up at the house with Ryan and a rusted-out 1955 baby blue Cadillac.

They had to get it towed into the driveway as the car hadn't run in almost a decade, but the boys had been taking a mechanic class at the local trade school just to fix this car up.

That entire summer was spent with drills and loud saws screaming from the garage. Nicole would come out and check on them every so often, but they were totally independent for the most part.

After a few weeks of consistent work, Cody and Ryan pulled the car out of the garage and took it on its inaugural drive around the neighborhood. It backfired time and time again, wouldn't go over ten miles an hour, and made the whole forest smell like a smogged-out factory, but the car moved.

This success lit a fire underneath the boys to keep working. They wanted to drive it into school on the first day of their senior year to make an impression. Cody had even welded a rack onto the back bumper that held both of their mountain bikes so they could take it to practice.

There were a few hiccups along the way, but a week before school started, they had gotten the Caddy up and running like new.

Just when Ryan had thought they were done, Cody pulled out a saw and told him what the plan was.

He wanted to fully remove the top of the car, allowing them to feel the wind blowing in their hair as they drove, impress all the ladies, and feel free.

Ryan knew what it was actually about, though. Cody was terrified of getting trapped in a car like his dad had, and being the good friend he was, Ryan just laughed and grabbed the other saw to get to work.

They had the top off within the hour, and the car was finally ready for its grand debut at school the following Monday.

That day started with a beautiful blue sky under which the boys drove to school in their new ride. It was as great a hit as they had hoped for. All their classmates were crowded around it before they could even park the car.

However, by the third period, the weather had taken a turn for the worse. Storm clouds gathered and started to release a torrential rainstorm.

The boys had known this could happen and had laid a tarp across the top of the car, figuring that would keep the rain out.

Instead, the rain simply weighed the tarp down and formed a liner that held the water inside the car, like a small swimming pool.

When they got to the car at the end of the day, the entire thing was full of water. Ryan opened the passenger door and water cascaded out, sweeping him entirely off his feet and onto the ground.

Cody laughed harder than ever at his best friend lying on the ground, flopping like a fish out of water. Ryan could only laugh along with him and hop straight back up.

They hopped in the car, and miraculously, it started right up.

Soaking wet with grins plastered across their faces, they pulled out of the parking lot and took the long way home.

By the time they pulled into Cody's driveway, the car had filled right back up with water, looking like a baby blue bathtub on wheels.

After that first debut, the car had never wanted to start up again, and despite their best efforts, it ended up back at the junkyard they had found it in.

This second Cadillac was Cody's hopeful attempt at getting another one up and running so he could take long drives without the fear of getting stuck inside.

Outside the garage, Cody had a more up-to-date Jeep Wrangler with its top off. No matter how much snow or rain there was, he barely ever put the top on, and if he did, it was either by the request of Sally or it was raining cats and dogs. Sometimes, he used just the soft top to keep the water out of his face when he drove.

"Oh, hey!" He set his tools down and ran over to kiss her.

Even after over a decade of dating and four years of marriage under their belts, the feeling of love filled the room every time these two were in it.

Sally laughed as Cody swept her off her feet and spun her around inside the garage. He nimbly avoided tools that lay on the ground and eventually brought her outside into the sun.

"Alright! Alright! Let me down!"

He sat her down gently. Everything he did when he was at home seemed gentle. When he was out racing, it was a completely different story.

Cody let out more laughter as he took a seat outside their garage and encouraged Sally to come over to him.

As he was laughing, there was another voice that got louder and louder until it was right in Cody's ear. "Daddy! Daddy!"

At four years old, Thomas had enough energy to power the entire neighborhood. His parents often joked about renting him out to the neighbors to get their power bill taken care of as well.

"Big man! What are you doing out here? I thought you were supposed to be in school today!"

"Dad! Come on, you know I already went to school! I just got home like thirty minutes ago, but you couldn't hear me. That saw's REAL loud! When can I try it?" His excitement carried further and further until he could barely contain it and Cody needed to grab him up off the ground just to calm him.

"Oh, wow. I've been out here that long, huh?"

Sally smiled and nodded. She knew he would still get everything else around the house done, but he never missed Thomas coming home from school.

"Well, I'm sorry, bud! I must have gotten lost in the work out here. I just really want to get that roof off. You know how it is. I just don't like being confined to small spaces. I need to feel the breeze, feel set free every time I hit the road!"

Thomas laughed as he wiggled around in Cody's arms. "I think the car is SO cool! But Dad, don't you have a big race tomorrow?"

He was young, but he was also right. Cody had one of the year's biggest races coming up in the morning. The magazines had all built him up to be the strongest competitor for this year's World Competition Race.

The interviews that he accepted were few and far between. He was busy with his job as a forest ranger and building his family; he didn't want mountain biking to be the only thing in his life. Regardless, he was the best, and everyone knew it.

They all called him the Michael Phelps of mountain biking. There were long articles discussing the crazy proportions of Cody's body and how the immensity of his legs allowed him to bike harder than anyone else out there.

"You know what? You're right! And I think that means it's time for ice cream! I'll race ya!"

Cody bolted off towards the door of the house, faked a fall, and rolled around on the ground as he let Thomas breeze past him. It was probably the only race that Cody ever lost or ever would lose.

That night, the three of them ate ice cream, relaxed on the couch, and spent their night laughing at each other's bad jokes. Their family was good at that. Cody never pushed them to follow a certain diet for his biking and never demanded rest on the night before a race.

He was playful with them, just like he was playful with everything in his life.

Even chopping the top off his old Cadillac was fun for him. Ryan and Sally laughed at him for it, but he didn't let that stop him.

His playfulness and determination carried right over to his mountain biking. In every interview he did, he talked about how these were his true superpowers. Yes, his legs were strong, but his ability to play and set his goals was even stronger.

The next day, they loaded up in the Wrangler early in the morning with three bikes on the rack attached to the hitch. Cody always liked to do a warmup with his family, and sometimes they even went for short rides after.

Thomas was taking quickly to the sport. Even at four years old, he already had proportions like his dad's. Cody certainly wouldn't stop him from pursuing the sport he loved more than almost anything else.

When all of the racers lined up to take off down the mountain, Cody didn't look a bit nervous. He was right next to Ryan, as he was for most of their races.

Cody flashed him a smile, and as soon as the first sound of the starter pistol came to the racers, Cody was yards ahead of everyone else.

Every race started this way, so none of the bystanders were too surprised. What started to catch their attention in the following moments was Matthieu Garnier, a French rider who was the only one that could possibly grab the title out of Cody's grips.

While Cody was fast and full of power, Matthieu rode like this was a ballet. Every turn he took was with calculated grace. Every jump was taken with perfect form. It was as if someone had turned the "How to Mountain Bike" book into human form and put it on the course that day.

As the race went on, the power that Cody was putting out wasn't enough to make up for all of the distance that Matthieu was cutting off with his technical skills. He gained on Cody through the densely treed section of the course, where most riders actually lost time.

The bright yellow of Matthieu's bike flashed in the edge of Cody's vision. He was just behind him, about to take the lead.

Cody's career was the highlight of every mountain biking forum online, every magazine that even barely mentioned bikes, and all the athletic publications that didn't.

There was a good reason for it, too. The racing lines that Cody took on were far from normal, even amongst his top competitors.

His first professional race was down a local trail that few riders took the time to pedal all the way up. The downhill was so littered with roots and large boulders that the technical riding skills needed were beyond most riders' abilities.

Cody, on the other hand, had taken his bike up this mountain when he was only 13 years old. He had gone there every week, falling and failing time and time again.

It was the place he went when he needed the challenge to take his mind completely off losing his dad.

Because of the years he'd spent on this mountain, the day that downhill race first popped up, he was the first to sign on to compete. He knew the twists and turns of the trail like he knew the back of his hand. Every turn and corner was no problem, just an opportunity for Cody to pick up and maintain more speed.

In that race, Cody had faced one of his most daring competitors, an Austrian named Edgar Mosig. Edgar was more famous in all of Europe than Cody was in his own home state, and Edgar was projected to win the race by a landslide.

Cody had decided he needed to come up with something new and interesting to up his chances of winning.

For the years he had been riding that trail, he had always noted one off-trail section that would cut almost a quarter-mile of riding completely from the ride.

The only problem was that the slick rock with ledges and gravel chunks splattered around the route was dangerous to walk around, let alone ride your bike on.

On the day of the race, Cody hadn't decided if he was going to try it out, but he knew that he would need to give it his all in order to possibly win.

Edgar started out of the gate faster than anyone Cody had ever gone up against, but Cody managed to stick closely behind him.

Through the first steep sections of the trail, Cody never let him out of sight and stayed only far enough back to stop the dirt from spraying in his face.

He took every chance there was to bring himself forward and overtake Edgar if he made a mistake, but he never made a mistake. Every turn was cornered perfectly, and every jump landed so smoothly that it seemed to speed him up rather than slow him down.

By the time the race approached the off-trail section that Cody had been considering the whole way down, he knew that he had no other choice but to take it if he wanted to win.

He veered hard to the right and soared off the trail and onto the slick rock that he'd been staring down for years.

His back tire immediately slid from under him, and he just barely caught his balance before pushing all his power into the pedals and moving forward.

Each and every ledge pushed him a few feet up and off the ground, barely missing the branches overhead. By taking each jump at full speed, he could miss the roots and gravel, which would force him to slow down considerably.

Everyone watching the race was in absolute awe at the moves he was pulling while cruising down the cliffside without a second thought.

He hit each bank with perfect precision and used his momentum to carry him forward down the untraveled trail.

The spot where he would hit the main race trail was a ten-foot drop with a sharp turn at the bottom of it. This was far more technical than the moves they included in most downhill races, and the likelihood of him crashing and losing the race was highly likely.

But when he hit that jump, he stayed solid and angled his bike perfectly so it was ready for the turn when it came.

Dirt sprayed from his back wheel, straight into the line of Edgar, who was just now approaching the spot Cody landed in.

He went on to win the race with only a few feet between his and Edgar's front tires. The world of mountain biking went wild, replays of Cody's daring stunt were all over the news, and he became a common name in the world of biking from that day forward.

So, as Matthieu was just about to catch up with him, he thought back to that first time he took a chance on himself and decided to try a daring move rather than take second place.

As the two racers came around the final curve of the course, Matthieu was close enough for Cody to reach out and grab him. If this was anything like the way he and Ryan used to ride, he would have cut right in front of him now, but Cody wanted to win this fair and square without any tricks.

Instead of getting in the way, Cody sent everything he had down his long legs. At the finish line, he could see Thomas and Sally screaming his name. He would do this for them. He would do this for his dad.

His bike inched forward to overtake Matthieu's as he pumped is legs down in the highest gear possible. Later, Sally would tell him all about the look on Matthieu's face at that moment. It was pure amazement and utter disbelief.

This was the kind of show that mountain bike fanatics around the world hoped for. Cody cruised out in front of Matthieu, eventually able to cut him off and block any chance of being passed.

The finish line was surrounded by local fans. Cody's old babysitter was there alongside his third-grade math teacher and the local pastor. Even Sarah, the girl who had a crush on him in high school, showed up.

He ripped through the red tape of the finish line, with Matthieu blasting through right behind him. He'd done it. He'd taken first in the World Championships.

Cody Long Legs, the bear chaser, had come in first place in the world. He tried to think of his dad and how proud he would have been as Thomas and Sally rushed him and took him into their arms.

His own thoughts were completely drowned out by the noise of the crowd.

The next day, Cody was back at work. The day before had been a complete whirlwind. They went out with the entire town to celebrate at Keeley's Pizza House, the little local grease joint, and then went home for a calm night.

Sally had encouraged Cody to take the day off work, but that would have meant staying home and cooped up indoors.

Cody liked his life as a park ranger. He got to go out and explore the trails. On most days, he and Ryan could leave their desks and do some patrols on their bikes.

It had ended up being the perfect job for Cody. He rarely had to be inside, and the rest of the rangers knew that he would be the first one to report to any emergencies. He was always itching to get outside.

That day, the rangers were discussing a black bear in the area that had gone into someone's camp and completely ransacked their stash of food. They were contemplating finding the bear to put it down, but Cody fought adamantly against that idea.

He proposed that they shut down that campground for the next few weeks and see if there were any other incidents. He would go out and check the area, make sure no human food was left behind, and hopefully, the bear would lose interest.

The other rangers were hesitant to shut down that campground as it was one of the more popular ones in the region. But Cody couldn't stand the thought of putting a bear down. It hadn't hurt anyone, and he thought the problem could be solved without any killing.

Eventually, everyone agreed to Cody's idea. He was hard to argue with.

"You're just as stubborn as your old man was," Phil, the oldest ranger around, pointed out.

"I'm going to take that as a compliment! But remember, I'm only twenty-six. I've got plenty of room to be more stubborn!" Cody joked with Phil often. They had known each other since Cody was born. Phil had stepped in to help out Nicole back when his dad passed away and was one of the reasons Cody still wanted to be a ranger.

"Hey, Ryan! You want to go ride out to that campsite and put up some signs with me?"

"Yeh! I could use some loosening up. That race yesterday left me completely wiped out."

"Ha, I know what you mean. Sally laughed at me as I struggled my way over to the shower this morning."

A few minutes later, they had grabbed their packs and tuned up their bikes for the ride. The campsite was one of the closer ones to the Ranger's Station, so they didn't have to push their legs too much after a big race day.

Ryan and Cody cruised downhill away from the little hut they had called their office for the past four years. Both of them had tried college but didn't have much interest in anything other than being in the forest with their bikes.

They rode these trails religiously. Every little curve was familiar to them, and they actually looked forward to the days when branches fell over the trails, giving them new obstacles to play around with before they had to head back and clean them up.

The past few days had been filled with discussions about the bear in the area. Part of Cody wondered if it was the same bear he and Ryan had nursed back to health years ago.

Most of him didn't want to believe that the cub he cared for was causing problems with the campers in the area. He couldn't stand the thought of her being the bear who might need to be put down.

That just meant he needed to do what he could to keep that from happening.

As the two of them got closer to the campground, they could see the signs of disturbance all around them. The bushes on the side of the trail were pushed down, branches were cracked, and there were scattered food wrappers in what would normally be pristine wilderness.

Cody took the lead, not slowing down too much. He wanted to get to the campsite and see the damage before cleaning everything up.

It all happened in a flash.

From behind him, he heard a quick, low growl and then the sound of a bike crash.

Cody had spooked the bear, which then jumped out onto the trail, right in front of Ryan. Ryan tried to swerve off the trail and go around, but the bear was massive, and the trail was cut through dense brush. There was nowhere to go.

By the time Cody could stop and turn around, Ryan was on the ground. He'd rolled over onto his stomach with his hands on his neck, just like they'd practiced in ranger training.

Cody weighed his options. He screamed at the bear with absolutely no response. He may as well have been shouting at the sky.

Without hesitation, he ran towards Ryan and the bear with his bear spray out and aimed right at them. He figured Ryan would forgive him for pepper spraying him to get rid of the bear.

Before he could pull the trigger, the bear turned on him.

Cody tried to avoid it, but there was really no chance that he was going to be faster than the bear standing two feet taller than him. That bear relied on its reflexes; Cody just hoped his own were enough.

The bear's paw came down and knocked the bear spray right out of his hands. It went flying towards Ryan, a few feet out of his reach.

Cody turned to try and get away, but he wasn't fast enough.

The bear reared up on two legs for an attack, its full weight coming down directly on Cody and bringing him to the ground.

Laying on the ground, face in the dirt, Cody was afraid. He knew the statistics. Most deaths were caused by black bears, not their grizzly cousins.

He felt the bear come down on him again. All of the wind came out of him, and he thought he heard a crunching noise. He didn't feel any pain. He couldn't really feel anything at all.

Then there was a sudden relief of pressure. The bear wasn't on top of him anymore, but he wasn't sure how.

He thought he could see two bears in his blurred vision, but he wasn't sure.

He could hear Ryan grab his radio out of his bag and call in to the station.

"We're down at the Fireside campsite, a quarter mile north of the outhouses and up the Fairy Ring Trail. Cody's down. Requesting emergency assistance immediately."

The Fairy Ring Trail. What a pleasant place to be, Cody thought as his world began to flicker in and out.

He could see Ryan coming to him behind the veil of his eyelids.

"You're gonna be alright, buddy. We've got search and rescue headed our way, and that bear's gone."

Cody tried to mumble a joke, something positive, anything at all. Nothing came out.

CHAPTER SIX

"Cody? Can you hear me?" Sally turned her head and shouted out to the hallway. "Doctor! Doctor! I think he's waking up!"

He could hear the words, but his eyes didn't want to open fully.

The beeping of – what was it? Hospital equipment? A car door slamming? No, that was a door opening. And that voice... I know that voice.

"It's me, honey. Sally. I'm here; everything's okay."

Sally. Sally and Thomas. That's right. My family.

"You were in an accident, but everything's alright. You're in the hospital. Can you hear me?"

Sally took his hand in hers. Almost as soon as she grabbed on, Cody squeezed. A smile of relief took over her worried face. "Thomas! Come over; I think he can hear me."

"Dad? Can you hear me? I'm right here for you." His voice was faint, hesitant almost. There was fear behind the bravery and tough attempt to be strong.

"Thom...Thomas?" Cody mumbled, clearly showing the strength it took to get the words out.

Thomas lit up. He glanced over at Sally, who was still sitting on the side of the hospital bed, a grin covering her face.

Slowly, Cody was able to open his eyes and take in the world around him. The smell of disinfectant flooded his senses at the same time that the bright fluorescent bulbs nearly blinded him. He couldn't wait to get outside.

"What...what happened?" He was still struggling to speak, but his curiosity and need to know what had happened were as alive as ever.

"There was an accident with a bear on the trail. Ryan's the one who should really tell you. He's the one that saved your life. All we did was sit here and wait for you to wake up."

Sally walked to the door and put her head into the hallway. She gestured towards the room, calling someone in.

Ryan's typical marine-like posture was slumped down. His arm was in a sling, and he had bandages covering his neck and part of his head.

It was the bags beneath his eyes that told the entire story, though. He hadn't slept since the accident. It had been nearly three days of waiting and hoping for Cody to come out of his deep sleep.

He slowly made his way over to Cody. Sally and Thomas switched places with him and stepped out into the hallway. There were parts of the story that Thomas should know, but he didn't need to see his dad relive the entire thing.

Cody could see the sadness inside Ryan. He sat on the end of the bed, looking at Cody without saying a word, seemingly frozen inside of his own head.

It was Cody who got the first words out.

"Ryan. I hear you saved my life, huh? Not too much of a surprise there. Man, I love you."

The corner of Ryan's mouth perked up for the first time since that ride.

"I've got to know what happened. Did you fight that bear off? I remember the ride, and I remember the bear charging me. Then the world just went black, and now here I am. What's the story?"

"Listen, Cody. It's not pretty. I don't really know what happened back there or really why it happened. You've got someone looking out for you; that's all I know. Neither of us should have made it out of there alive."

Cody laughed. He was trying to make Ryan feel better about it all. He knew it wasn't Ryan's fault, but he also knew Ryan. He was blaming himself for the entire thing.

"Oh, I'm sure my dad put in a good word for me. That man was always so charming. He could have talked the bear into going for ice cream in the middle of attacking me."

Ryan smiled but was still quiet.

Cody reached over and nudged Ryan's shoulder. "You're killing me here! Let's hear the whole thing. What went down? Why aren't I lying in a pine box next to my old man right now?"

Ryan took in a deep breath. It felt like forever until he finally let it out.

"Alright. Well, I'm not really sure what went down the whole time. I got knocked down first, but you had to be the hero and come back. I guess you thought we could make a run for it or something. I don't know. But the bear wasn't about to let us off the hook."

He paused and took another breath, looking towards the window. Cody started thinking there was something he didn't know that had gone worse than he thought.

"The bear just...launched onto you. It was relentless, smacking you over and over. I didn't know what to do. My bear spray was tossed into the bushes, and I knew I couldn't just fight it off of you."

He shifted on the bed, moving his nervous energy around a bit before continuing the story.

"It all happened so fast, but another bear showed up and body-slammed the first one right off you. Then that one was pissed. They wrestled around for what seemed like ages. Eventually, they just kind of took off into the bushes, but the bear that saved you hung back for a minute."

Cody was shocked. "What? It just stood there, looking at us?"

"Not at us. Looking at you. I don't know, but I think that bear knew you."

"No way. It couldn't be...could it? You think it's possible that bear was the one we took in all those years ago? How old would it be by now? Fifteen? That's crazy."

"Maybe it was, maybe it wasn't. But that bear saved both of our lives. I guess we're even now."

Cody remembered the feeling of knowing that Ryan was hiding something. "What else is there? That's the story, but why are you being so weird? We're both fine. I woke up, didn't I? We're not in some sick and twisted dream or anything, right?"

"Cody, I don't think I should be the one–"

"The one that what?"

"The one that tells you what happened."

"You just did! The bear saved me. We both almost died, it was crazy, but we're okay."

"Well, we're alive."

Cody knew there was more to this. "Yeh, we're alive. What else, Ryan?"

Ryan hesitantly got up off of the bed and walked to the door. "Let me just get Sally."

"No way, man! Tell me what's going on." Cody was starting to get mad. Cody never got mad.

He tried to turn on the bed. His top half twisted to the right, but nothing else moved. His brain was telling his legs to lift up and over so he could stand up and face Ryan.

No matter what he told his legs, they wouldn't listen.

It struck him like a freight train. Fear and panic washed over him like the bore tide he watched as a kid.

"My legs! What's going on? Ryan? Sally!"

Sally rushed in next to him and held him in her arms.

"No. It can't be like this! Anything else, anything at all. My legs? They won't move! Why won't they move?"

"Oh, Cody." Sally tried to talk to him, but he kept rambling on. He went into a mode she had never seen him in throughout the almost twenty years they had known each other.

When he wouldn't calm down on his own, Sally called for the nurse to come in.

In moments, a nurse came into the room with a doctor right behind him. The doctor, a woman barely older than Cody, came in and took a seat. Cody just stared at her.

"What? Is this where you tell me I'll have years of physio, but eventually, I can walk if I put my all into it? What's going on?"

The doctor took a moment before speaking.

"No, Cody. I'm afraid it's not like that. I'm really sorry, Cody. There was a break in your spine. Multiple thoracic vertebrae were completely smashed. We did our absolute best, but there was too much damage. I'm afraid you'll likely never walk again."

Never walk again? Cody thought, frozen in fear. *Never? But what about biking? What about the park? How will I play with Thomas? Who am I without my legs?*

"I know it's a lot to take in. It's going to be a long journey, but I assure you—"

Cody lost it.

"Get out! Everyone, just get out! I don't want to see anyone! I don't want to hear this!"

He grabbed his cup of water, threw it toward the doctor, and turned to look for something else to grab.

Sally ushered the doctor and nurse out of the room before trying to come back to comfort him.

"I said, get out!"

"Cody, honey. It's going to be okay. We're going to make this work."

"Didn't you hear her? I'm never going to walk again! How is that okay? How am I okay?"

"I know, but you still have us. You still have Ryan."

"What I want is my legs back!"

Sally took a breath and tried to think of something to say to calm him down.

But Cody's face wasn't his own anymore. Sally saw a different person in that hospital bed, and she did what she never thought she would do. She walked away.

****

Cody spent the next two weeks lying in his hospital bed, barely talking to anyone. Ryan and Sally took turns by his side; there was never a moment that he was alone for too long.

Thomas would come and visit, jumping around on his hospital bed, trying to get his dad to laugh. Sometimes it worked, and Cody could smile along with Thomas. Sometimes it didn't.

There was an obvious difference in Cody's everyday demeanor. He used to be charming, funny, and so highly energetic. Now, he went through slumps where he wouldn't do much more than lay in bed and look at the ceiling.

Ryan took him outside in his wheelchair. He seemed happier during these short trips, but the moment they were back inside, he sank back into a depression.

Every day he asked about going home.

The time finally came that the doctor signed off on his discharge, and Sally came to bring him home.

Ryan and Sally loaded him into Ryan's Range Rover with the wheelchair in the back to finally head home.

The drive was silent. No one felt fully sure of how to talk about what was going on and what Cody's life was going to look like.

It was a massive shift from what their car rides used to be, the car's stereo blasting and everyone laughing.

Today was different. Cody wanted to get home, away from the hospital where the earth-shattering news had broken his spirit.

When they pulled into the cabin's driveway, Thomas ran straight up to the car and started asking his dad if he wanted to see the new tricks he had learned on his bike. In the past, it was always Cody's favorite thing to do with Thomas.

"I'm sorry, buddy. Not today," Cody said through a clenched jaw. He couldn't bear the thought of watching anyone, even his own kid, do the thing he used to love the most. Not yet.

"Would you run and grab me some blankets, though? I'd like to sit out on the porch. Don't think I can go inside just yet."

"Yeh! Alright! We can sit there and maybe play cards, or we can look at the birds like we used to do before I learned how to ride!" Thomas was off in a heartbeat, running upstairs to get every blanket the house had to offer.

Sally seemed a bit unsure. "Are you positive you don't want to come in and get comfortable? Try to get some rest?"

"No. I need to be outside." He didn't mean to come off so harshly, but Sally looked defeated and didn't ask any questions after that.

They set him up on the front porch with blankets and a small space heater for when the evening set in. Sally knew he would be alright; he had always preferred being outside, and there had been plenty of nights she had essentially dragged him in to go to sleep.

Ryan went home after helping Cody get comfortable on the couch that was set up on the porch. He wanted to stay, but his girlfriend and their dog were probably starting to miss him after so much time at the hospital. Plus, Sally, Thomas, and Cody needed this time alone to start seeing what their new life was going to be like.

That night, Sally called and ordered takeout from the little Thai restaurant that an old friend of theirs had opened years ago. The food was only okay, but Cody always liked to joke about supporting a friend through a mouthful of mediocre pad thai.

Thomas brought out the binoculars and the little green Audubon book his dad had gotten him for his fourth birthday. Any time after a big race, Cody sat and watched the birds with him, his legs too tired to move.

Now, his legs wouldn't ever move again. But he still made an effort to act excited about the song of a finch or sparrow coming from the trees that surrounded their home.

They sat this way for a while, listening to the birds, devouring egg rolls, and not saying much.

Eventually, Sally told Thomas it was time for him to get upstairs and go to sleep.

"But Mom, I want to stay out here with Dad! We can get the second couch set up, and I'll be fine!"

Sally hesitated and looked to Cody for an answer. "Sorry, little man. Not tonight. You've had a long day, and this porch is littered with sweet and sour sauce. You'd have little raccoons and mice crawling all over you in no time."

"Oh, fine. But maybe tomorrow I'll be able to! I'll clean the porch up and everything. I swear!"

"We'll see about tomorrow when tomorrow comes. Goodnight, buddy. I love you." Cody turned and went back to staring deep into the forest as if Thomas had already run upstairs.

After Thomas was asleep in his bed, Sally came back out to sit with Cody.

For a few minutes, they enjoyed the silence. Sally was surprised when it was Cody that spoke first.

"I don't know what I'm going to do. I don't know who I even am at this point. I can never race my bike again. I can't be a ranger. Hell, I can barely even play with my own kid."

He paused and took a breath. Sally could tell there was a mass of emotions welling up inside of him, but he was doing better at managing those tonight.

"It's just, how am I supposed to move past this? I'm so lost. Confused. And above everything else, I'm just pissed. What did I do? I tried to save Ryan's life and lost my own! What am I going to do, Sal?"

Cody lost it. He buried his head in Sally's shoulder and stayed there, sobbing. She didn't have words that could fix this.

Maybe there were magic words out there. Maybe there was a chance for Cody to find a new life. But right now, no one really knew what that could possibly be.

CHAPTER SEVEN

"When we take a look at the ostrich, the ratio of weight to size is nowhere near that of the chickadee or any other flying bird for that case."

The lecture hall was half empty today, which was better than most days. Professor Reilley hardly noticed. He was so caught up and enthralled by his own teaching that the students were only there as a way for him to get paid.

"But, the ostrich has these massive legs, allowing it to reach speeds up to forty-three miles per hour!"

Professor Reilley paced back and forth across the front of the lecture hall while gesturing toward his complicated drawings pinned up on the board.

His black suede jacket trailed behind him, making his dark hair and thick black eyebrows pop out even more than normal. His sharp features could be intimidating, but when he started to talk about birds, everything softened and a new light radiated from his face.

"Now, the ostrich has obviously traded the remarkable talent of flight for the ability to run on land. If you then take a look at the penguin, it has made similar adaptations in regard to its swimming prowess."

Most of his students were slouched in their chairs, barely paying attention. One surprised Reilley by putting her hand in the air.

"Professor? I thought we were going to be covering the avian kingdom and the ways their seven defining characteristics have been put into place in different environments across the world."

Reilley was put off by this, but managed to respond rather than dive back into his normal weight and size ratio spiel.

"Well, yes. I suppose you're right. Forgive me, but I do believe the weight to size ratio and a bird's ability to take flight is directly linked to the seven classifying characteristics."

"And I totally agree!" The student seemed a bit embarrassed by her confronting question but continued to push. "But we also talked about this last week. I mean, you made us read your book on it. Isn't it time to move on to something else?"

"That's what everyone keeps telling me. It's time to move on to something else. Leave all of your work behind. Biology is moving forward and you should too."

He continued to trail off, talking more to himself than anyone else in the room.

When he noticed the students were still there, he dismissed the class early and headed to his office.

Stacked on his desk was a collection of newspapers and magazines, all surrounded by his chaotic sprawling of notes and books on birds and their evolutionary history. He threw the stack of essays he'd collected earlier next to those from last week he had yet to grade.

He sank into his office chair and took a moment to stare out the window behind him. His prized pair of Celestron binoculars sat on the window ledge, primed and ready for any sighting to come his way.

He'd seen a great variety of birds come through the university's campus in his tenure there as a biology professor. The sky was always active with the Downy woodpeckers, the summertime hummingbirds, and his personal favorite, crows.

In his opinion, crows were one of the most underrated birds out there. They could grow to a massive size and still dominate the skies. Of course, they were nothing like the great bustards he had seen during his sabbatical in Spain, but no other birds were that big and still capable of flight.

Today, the sky and the trees were quiet. Thanks to the incoming storm, the birds had all sought shelter, which told him to stay inside that day.

Since he wasn't going anywhere for a while, he started rifling through the newspapers that had stacked up over the week.

It was an old habit of his dad's that he had picked up. He loved reading the news from different parts of the state and even across the country. His father had always told him to broaden his perspective of the world, and small town local news had a way of bringing stories to his life that he would otherwise have missed.

He leafed through the first paper, reading about a cat that had become the mayor of a small town just east of where he'd grown up. The next paper featured a new fountain that was being installed in memoriam of a war hero who had called that town his home.

These were the typical stories he came across every week. He enjoyed the small oddities as they always took his mind away from the typical stress and constant turning of gears inside his head.

Then he turned the page, and there was a half-page story on a professional mountain biker who had just had a life-threatening and career-ending injury. The story told him that this man would never walk again.

He read the story over and over. Cody McCully was young, athletic, and seemed to have been in the wrong place at the wrong time. Really, it seemed like he was lucky to be alive, seeing as a second bear had supposedly saved him from the first.

Cody McCully was exactly the person that Professor Reilley had been looking for.

That was when the professor's mind took back over. He immediately opened his laptop and started looking for any other information on this young man that he could find. He found countless stories about his success as a mountain biker, how he came to have the nickname Cody "Long Legs", and a brief obituary for his father from almost two decades prior.

He found contact information for Cody's wife, Sally, and had to restrain himself to wait before making the call. This was his perfect opportunity. A man with a real athletic gift with a huge amount of his body mass in his legs? There wasn't a better shot out there.

If this was going to work out for the professor, he needed to do it right. So he kept looking into everything he could find out about Cody's past. He wanted to approach this with caution, not wanting to scare him away.

He stayed in his office for the rest of the day, the essays going untouched. All he could do was watch videos of Cody on his bike, read more about the incident, and try to figure out his plan.

****

Sally and Thomas had spent most of their time on the porch with Cody over the past few weeks since his accident. He refused to come inside most of the time except for the two times he had tried to take a bath.

Cody had changed since the attack. He looked exhausted every single day, despite rarely doing anything but sitting and staring out into the woods.

Not only was he tired, but he also didn't talk much. He could put on a show for Thomas, but every time his son went inside or to bed, Cody withdrew back into himself almost instantly. Sally could barely get through to him.

The three of them were on the porch working their way through a 500-piece puzzle that Cody's mother had sent over from her new place in Southern California. When it was put together, it was meant to be a giant sun reflecting off the ocean.

Cody's mom had visited right after the accident, but she had gotten a job far away right after Cody graduated from high school. She had gotten remarried to Jeff, a man Cody thought was "good enough" but had never fully connected with.

Instead of staying for very long, she sent small gifts like this puzzle, hoping that some sunshine would help Cody brighten up.

So far, it wasn't working.

Thomas clicked another piece into place and did what he called his 'happy dance' before looking for another piece to celebrate with.

That was one of the few things that could get a smile out of Cody these days. Thomas had always done his "happy dance," but the "quiet song" had come along after Cody's accident. It was a small thing, but enough to temporarily get Cody's spirits up.

"Dad! I bet I can get this tree done today. It's kinda like I'm growing it! From the trunk on up!"

"You betcha, Thomas. You keep working on it. Your grandma is going to be so excited to hear all about you growing that tree on your own."

From inside, Sally's phone started ringing.

"I bet that's her right now. Sally, would you mind grabbing it? I would, but you know." He gestured at his legs, completely immobile. "I might not make it there in time." He faked a laugh, trying his best to be better for Thomas.

"Of course, hun. I'll be right back."

Sally hopped up and ran inside, snatching the phone up on the fourth or fifth ring.

"Hello?"

From the other end of the line, she could make out a man's voice, but it was breaking up badly.

"I'm sorry, let me get outside, there's a way better signal up by the treehouse."

She ran outside and made her way to the clearing by the treehouse. It was where they had to take most of their calls, which is how they liked it.

"Okay, is that better?"

Now she could fully hear the man speaking on the other end of the line. He spoke quickly, seemingly excited and a bit nervous.

"Hello. Is this Sally? This is Professor Reilley from Gemboldt University. I'm a biologist and I'm calling about your husband."

"Uh, hi, Professor. How can I help you?"

"Well, I'm actually calling because I have a proposition. I think your husband is going to be the perfect fit for the job."

Sally hesitated, unsure of what this man wanted from Cody. "I'm sorry, but you must not have heard. He's been in an accident recently. My husband can't even walk. He barely leaves his spot on the porch anymore."

"Exactly! What I'm offering is a chance for your husband to discover something new. I'm offering your husband the chance to be great again. I want to teach your husband how to fly!"

She laughed a bit, unsure of what the Professor was talking about, but he continued on.

"Listen, I know it sounds crazy, but I know it can work. Just let me talk to him for a few minutes and I guarantee that I can give him his hope back. I can give him the courage to get back to living and a purpose to move from that front porch of yours."

She hadn't been able to get Cody to move for weeks. At this point, she was willing to try almost anything, and what harm could a single phone call do?

"Okay, fine. Let me go bring him the phone. Just wait a minute."

She bounced up to the front porch and told Cody the phone was for him.

"Who is it?"

"I don't really know. It's some professor from that university out near Spokane, I think. He said he wants to talk to you. Something about you being the perfect fit, I don't really know."

Rather than looking confused, Cody actually seemed intrigued. "Alright, give me just a second and I'll wheel myself over to the treehouse so I can actually hear him."

Cody hauled himself off the couch and over into his wheelchair and brought himself over to the top of the small, three-step staircase leading into the house.

Last week he had asked Ryan over to help him and Thomas with a project. Together, they built a small ramp down from the steps and it was Cody's new favorite thing to do. He would get a "running" start at times and launch himself down the ramp, his own little bit of adrenaline.

He had a bigger plan for paving a path through their woods so he could get around. He went back and forth between paving the ground and just building an off-roading wheelchair so he could tackle some of the trails he used to bike down. That was a long way off, though.

Cody wheeled himself over to Sally where she stood with the phone and shrugged to her. "Alright, let's see what this is all about, I guess."

He grabbed the phone and brought it to his ear as Sally walked back to the porch. He had no idea that it would be a phone call that would completely reroute his life.

"Hello?"

"Ah, Cody? Pleasure to meet you. My name is Professor Reilley. I'm calling with a slight proposition."

"Uh, okay? What exactly are you talking about?"

"Let me start by saying, I'm terribly sorry about your accident. It must be incredibly difficult. But, I want to give you a second chance. Cody, I want to make it possible for you to fly."

Cody was completely unimpressed. A chance to fly? Who was this stranger calling with such a ridiculous idea? He almost hung up right there.

"Alright, funny man. I get it. I'm down and out. There's nothing left for me. You don't need to make me into a laughing stock."

"That's not what I'm trying to do here. Hear me out. I have a plan, and I know it can work. I can get you flying. I've been studying birds, their body proportions, the way they've evolved and developed the muscles necessary for flight. I believe that you are a perfect fit."

"You think a six-foot-three man with legs that don't work is your perfect fit to fly?"

"Well, no. That's the catch. I can get you flying. I swear by it. But the legs, they need to go."

"What the hell are you talking about? My legs need to go? I'm not cutting off my legs just to be your little lab rat, sir."

"I know it sounds difficult. But the surgery is simple. I have the funding for the project; you don't need to pay anything. If we get rid of the weight from your legs, you'll be light enough to take flight. You'll be the first person to ever fly!"

Cody was still uninterested. "You think people haven't ever been in a plane before? Come on, Doc. People fly all the time."

"No, this is different. You will be the one doing the flying. You have to power it all. You're in full control, just like a bird."

"I don't know about this. You're asking me to completely get rid of my legs, all for what? A chance to maybe flap some sheets around on my arms and get laughed at? The cripple who thought he could fly?"

"It's much more intensive than that. You would have to be on a strict diet and consistently work on your muscle mass to get the weight ratio to the perfect number in order to maintain flight. This isn't something that many people could do, with or without legs."

Sally was looking out at Cody from the porch, tilting her head as if to ask what was happening.

"Listen, I don't know about this. It sounds a little far-fetched. No offense, but I think I'm going to have to at least take a little bit to think about this."

"Yes, of course. Take all the time you need. I will send my information over to you and your wife soon. You can take a look at the idea. It'll all be there in the email. I've put together a massive presentation just for this moment. I didn't know if I would ever find the right person and I know you're it."

It felt a little kooky to be told that he was the perfect fit now that he'd completely lost everything he had worked so hard for. In a way, there was a bit of hope growing inside of Cody. Maybe this was all real, maybe it actually was as good as it sounded.

"Okay, well, thank you for your time. I'll be in touch," said the professor before hanging up.

Partially stunned, Cody hung up the phone and just stared over at Sally. She came over to help him get back up the porch. He still hadn't gotten the strength to roll himself up the ramp completely.

Thomas looked up from the puzzle as his dad came back to the couch. "Who was that, dad?"

"I'm not sure, buddy. I think it might be someone that's either a little crazy or maybe a bit brilllant."

That night, Cody and Sally discussed Reilley's proposal. Sally's immediate reaction was that it was completely insane.

"This man can't just chop off your legs! That's not how that works. Isn't the surgery dangerous? What if it doesn't work and then you're just without your legs?"

"Can't hurt to be without my legs, right? It's not like they're doing much for me anyway."

She looked at him in disbelief. "You're really thinking of doing this, aren't you?"

"Well, yeah, I think so. It could give me something to do. It sounds like it would require a lot of time at the gym, which I know Ryan would love. Plus, look at me, Sally. I'm pathetic. I've been sitting on that porch just wallowing in my own misery for the past month. Is that good for Thomas? To see his dad like that? Shouldn't he see me going out and chasing dreams, trying to be the man I can be, even without my legs?"

Sally didn't know how to respond. She just laid her head on Cody's shoulder. She couldn't argue with the fact that this was the most alive she had seen him in the entire time since the surgery.

Plus, he was right. If this got him back to being his old self, wouldn't it all be worth it?

They spent the rest of the evening looking at the plans and proposal that Reilley had sent over immediately after the phone call.

The next day, Cody called him up and told him that he was in.

CHAPTER EIGHT

St. John's Memorial Hospital was only an hour's drive from their house, but both Sally and Cody felt like they'd traveled ages to get there.

It had been three and a half months since Cody and Professor Reilley had come to an agreement about performing the surgery and learning to fly. Cody had dedicated that time to three things: starting his diet and fitness plan with the professor, researching the history of human flight and reading over the journals the professor provided him on the evolution of birds, and spending time with Thomas and Sally.

Things had started to turn around for him in the last several months. His general mood was lifted, he moved around more, and he rarely talked about the life he once had.

Sally and Ryan both attributed this shift to his newfound purpose and the physical work that came along with it. Ryan and Cody were at the gym four times a week, and when he wasn't at the gym, he was working out at home.

In the gym, Cody followed a strict upper body regiment that was designed by the best fitness advisors on the planet. The workouts aimed to build muscle while preventing weight gain from too much growth.

Ryan was crucial to everything that Cody did over those few months. He picked him up from his house, brought him to the gym, and helped him create workout programs focused on his upper body.

He also noticed a shift in Cody's ability to move around independently. He was willing to try getting out of the chair and into the car on his own. He racked his own weights and got himself onto the various workout benches.

Each time the two of them came home, Ryan reported to Sally on Cody's progress. They both started to think the whole "taking flight" project was actually worth it.

And Thomas. Thomas just couldn't get enough of it once he found out his dad's plan. He constantly was showing his dad videos from the internet of people building homemade contraptions and trying to take flight.

In school, he started his own report on the Wright brothers and told the class that his dad was likely to be even more famous than they were because he would fly on his own.

Despite all this progress, there was a lingering feeling of anxiety in the family. They knew the surgery was coming quickly.

They had expected it to take about six months to schedule a surgery, but the professor had pulled strings to have it as fast as possible. That's how they ended up in the hospital only a few months later, ready to say goodbye to Cody's legs.

"I guess they won't be able to call me Long Legs anymore, huh?"

Sally threw him a forced smile.

"I wonder what they'll call you now. Birdman? Cody the Condor? Can't you see the headlines? From bikes to birds, Cody McCully takes to the sky!"

Cody laughed a full-hearted laugh that Sally felt like she hadn't heard in a long time. "That's right! I bet we'll have to start communicating with carrier pigeons again! Or maybe I can get a job as one."

The two of them passed jokes back and forth, lightening the mood while they waited for the doctors to come and bring him into surgery. It felt like the old times when they were first falling in love. There wasn't a care in the world. Neither of them even stopped to think about what an odd situation they were in.

"Okay, Cody, I think that's the doctor coming in now. I love you. Both Professor Reilley and I will be here when you wake up."

"Hey, Sally. Just don't worry, okay? Routine surgery, that's all it is." He smiled his trophy-winning smile, the one that had been posted in papers for years up until now.

As the doctors wheeled him away, he shouted back to her. "I love you! Maybe return those jump ropes we just got, though!"

Sally couldn't help but laugh. Then he was gone. The silence washed over her, and all she could do was wait.

–

The familiar beeping of the heart rate monitor and the smell of a sterile hospital room was what Cody woke up to four days later.

Huh, this feels familiar, he thought before trying to move at all.

In a way, he could still feel his legs, and he wondered if the surgery hadn't happened or if something had gone wrong. That feeling of brief panic forced him back into this world as he opened his eyes.

Where his legs would have normally pushed up the bedsheet, there was nothing. He ripped the sheet off from on top of him and had a look.

The feeling of his legs was still there, but his legs were completely gone.

Then he noticed that Professor Reilley was sitting in the corner chair, a book opened up on his lap with his eyes closed and head back.

"Hey! Prof! Wake up; it's good news!"

The Professor came to and opened his eyes to see Cody sitting upright in bed.

"Whoa! Lay back down, Cody. You're on a lot of meds right now, and we don't want you ripping open those stitches."

"I know, I know, but look! My legs are gone! They did it!"

"Yes. Yes, they did. The surgery was a total success without a single hitch. They just induced sleep for the past few days so you would miss the worst of the pain. But remember, you're on a lot of drugs right now, so you need to stay still."

Cody listened and laid back down, pulling the sheet back over him.

"Where's Sally at? I want to see her and Thomas. They should probably know I'm alright, right?"

"Yes, of course. I will call her as soon as we're done talking. She just went home to get Thomas. They expected you to wake up soon, and she wanted him to be here for that. That woman hasn't left this room for more than a bathroom break in the last four days. You've got yourself a saint."

Cody didn't have anything to say to that, but the professor barely gave him a chance to speak anyway.

"Now listen, the average human leg is between 16 and 17 percent of your total weight. The beauty about you is how much longer your legs were than average. Each one of your legs accounted for closer to 20 percent of your total body weight. That means we've successfully removed almost 40 percent of your weight. You're almost to the perfect weight!"

"What do you mean, almost? I'm almost half what I used to weigh, and that's still not enough?"

"Well, you remember the numbers. You still need to drop some weight to be able to actually get up in the air. I got them to put you on a special diet for the rest of your time in the hospital. Low-glycemic foods only. Your body will naturally burn more fat this way and get rid of whatever else you have left while you can't work out much."

Cody was obviously a bit disappointed; his previous hospital experiences, when he got his tonsils out at age twelve and when he had his back accident, had been made up of jello and ice cream.

"Alright, I guess I can do that."

"Yes, Cody. You can! You must! According to my projections, you can be back at the gym within two weeks' time, so long as you're careful with your stitches. Until then, I've brought more weights to your house, and you can do some light lifting there. We can have you up in the air before the summer ends!"

"Before the summer ends? Isn't it already April? That doesn't give us much time at all. I don't even know how to function without my legs yet."

"Yes, yes," he responded with his normal impatient but driven tone. "But you will learn. You are a fast learner, and I believe you can do this. You must."

"I must? Or else what?"

"Or else, the summer ends, and you are unable to fly until next year! Our window is closing, and this is the year!"

Cody resigned and told the professor he was feeling tired again. He woke up to a meteor of pressure coming his way. He had two months to fully recover and learn how to fly?

He decided he would sleep until Sally and Thomas got there. They would know how to calm him down, not put even more pressure on him.

He dozed off and started to dream of birds.

In his dreams, he saw himself as one – not as a graceful swan or a powerful hawk, but as an ostrich trying to pick up speed and fly with no success.

He tried flying, but over and over, he couldn't get off the ground. When he looked down, his feet were completely gone.

Then the bigger monsters came into his dream space. From the forests behind him emerged a massive lion. As it ran towards him, it screamed, "You must! You must fly!"

He turned his head to the cliff behind him. No matter how hard he flapped his wings, he couldn't get off the ground, so he settled for his only option.

He fell off the cliff.

The fall down was long, and he kept trying to get his wings unfolded to stop his fall. One wing was open, turning him in one direction, but the other wouldn't open up. The ground got closer and closer.

He was about to hit the ground. There was no stopping it.

"Cody!"

Cody startled awake, covered in sweat. Sally stood above him, holding his arms in place.

"Cody, you're okay. I'm right here. Just breathe."

"What? What's going on?"

"It's okay. You're okay. We're still just in the hospital." Sally let go of his arms and sat down on the bed. "You were just thrashing around. I didn't want you to rip open the stitches."

"I...I think I just had a bad dream. I'm okay."

"Dad!"

Thomas ran in from the hallway, a bag of chips in his hands that he immediately dropped to the ground.

Cody hugged his son and kissed his wife. His family was here now. There may be a lot of pressure to fly, but his family would always take him in, flying or not.

＊＊＊＊

After a few weeks at home, Cody was already back in the gym with Ryan. Now, they were there almost every single day of the week.

On his new restrictive diet, Cody was losing weight quickly but building the necessary muscle as well. He felt stronger than he ever had and looked like he had been going to the gym his entire life.

Ryan helped push him to his limits and then past them. Every time Cody wanted to quit, Ryan reminded him why he was doing this.

Cody tried to explain it, but he always struggled with both Ryan and Sally. He thought the idea of flying was alright, but he was pursuing the feeling of being purposeful. He wanted to be set free from his new limits without legs. If he could fly, he could do anything.

This drive pushed him through the rigorous workouts they did every day. He was amazed by the variety of upper body workouts you could do when you never had to worry about leg day.

Even at home, he was training. With Thomas's help, he turned an old stationary bike into an arm-powered bike. He could use the pedals with his hands instead of his feet.

This is what he did almost all night, even after getting home from the gym. If the family was on the porch, he pedaled outside. Even on movie nights, he watched while pedaling.

There was a fire inside him that couldn't be put out.

Then, two months after the surgery, Professor Reilley showed up at their house. It was time to do Cody's final weigh-in.

It wasn't a very flattering process. They had to use an old cattle scale to weigh Cody accurately, and he felt like he was headed for slaughter rather than flight.

Regardless, when the scale finally registered, they all celebrated.

Cody hit his target weight and was under it by almost a pound.

Cody couldn't have been happier hearing this. He'd never tried harder for something in his entire life. Even in his peak days of mountain biking, he was still only training four days a week. Now, this was his life. He needed to meet this goal.

Sally was happy for Cody, but she also worried about him. He was skinnier than he'd ever been, even though he was covered in lean and wiry muscle. He looked more like an addict than an athlete without a single ounce of fat on his body.

Every time she had expressed this to him, he'd gotten upset. He would explain again why he was doing what he was doing. His theory was that he could prove to the professor that he could fly, and then he could eat real food and still be able to fly.

But for now, he was withering away and all Sally could do was support him.

After the weigh-in, Professor Reilley explained the next steps of their journey before heading out.

"So, tomorrow we can go to my office. I can take you there myself. Sally, you and Thomas are obviously more than welcome to join."

"Thank you, Professor."

"Of course. Then we will start to get you fitted for the wingsuit. I have done a lot of work with my engineers, but I think there will be adjustments that we will need to make before you fit into it perfectly."

"Okay. Sounds interesting, and then we fly. When will it be? The first flight?"

"I think sometime next week is a possibility, and I have a spot in mind. Have you ever heard of Mora Point? It's only an hour north of your hometown."

"No, I don't think so. We haven't spent much time up there." Cody always seemed a bit embarrassed by how little he'd traveled inside his home state.

"That's okay. It's a good location for our first flying attempt. There's a large hill with a decent driveway that I think you should be able to gain speed on."

"A driveway? Am I going to be on top of the car or something?"

At this point, Sally looked a bit uneasy, but he continued on.

"A car? No, of course not! This is about human flight. We don't need motors! Think of it like a skateboard. It will hold onto you until you are lifted upward by the aerodynamic properties of your wings. You will need to reach approximately 20 miles per hour to get off the ground."

Though Sally was unsettled, Cody's face lit up. Moving fast on wheels was his sport. This only made him more excited for the following week.

"Alright, Prof. I'm ready for it. I know it. Let's do this thing."

Professor Reilley made some final remarks before getting back in his car and heading to a nearby hotel.

That night, the McCully family sat together in near silence. They listened to the night fall upon them, all while there was an obvious feeling of change approaching. That change was coming, and it was coming fast.

CHAPTER NINE

At five o'clock the morning of Cody's long-awaited first flight, the McCullys hopped in the car with Ryan and started driving.

The professor had wanted the whole team to be in place no later than 7 a.m. He was increasingly strict about the time frame as the date approached.

He told Cody over and over that the winds were in their favor before noon, but once the afternoon came, the winds changed direction and would make the flight impossible. Cody and his family agreed to the early start.

Thomas was potentially the most excited out of everyone. He wore his Superman cape on top of his dad's old biking jersey, which he had worn when Cody won the World Competition Race less than a year earlier.

The four of them started off silently in the car, Thomas asleep and the rest of them sipping on their coffee, contemplating what was ahead of them.

Sally broke the silence twenty minutes in.

"Maybe I'm being stupid here, but how exactly do you even land?"

Cody laughed. "You know what? I'm not really sure. I guess I thought I'd just figure it out when I got to it!"

"We're not going to strap wheels up on your stomach like an airplane, right? I mean, maybe that's a good idea to bring up to the professor before the flight, huh?"

"Maybe that's exactly what we should do! Soon enough, I'll be on par with the commercial airlines and charging thousands per trip for this first-class seat."

The three of them laughed hard enough that it woke Thomas up.

"What did I miss? Are we already there?"

Ryan knuckled Thomas's hair and bumped him on the shoulder. "Nah, buddy. We've barely left! You best go back to sleep, and we'll be there by the time you wake up."

"Hey! You're just trying to make me miss all the fun!"

Regardless of what he said, Thomas's head fell back, and he was back asleep in zero seconds flat.

"Man, does that boy know how to sleep. No idea where he got that from. I remember getting calls from you to come over at like seven in the morning and you telling me that your mom had made you wait an hour to even call!" Ryan reached up and shook Cody by the shoulders playfully.

With all the playfulness and joking aside, the car went back to a somber feeling. They realized that they had no idea how Cody would land or what was going to happen.

Cody was the only one that could hold on to an optimistic feeling. He had to; otherwise, he had no idea what all of his work over the last few months had been for. Plus, he had cut his legs off for this. He was going to see it through.

He was going to fly.

The car pulled up to Mora Point around an hour later. The only other person around was Professor Reilley and his Volkswagen bus that looked like it had come right out of the '70s.

He waved them over towards his van and pointed to a small parking spot out of the way of the asphalt road.

"We need that clear! You see that? It's your runway, Cody!" He shouted at them with an energy that was out of place for 6:30 in the morning.

The professor helped Cody out of the car and into his chair before wheeling him over to the viewpoint.

Mora Point was a bluff that overlooked over 3,000 acres of forest, and the exposure took Cody by surprise.

"You're not hoping for me to fly out over that now, are you? That might be a big jump for my first flight, Prof."

"No, Cody. Of course not. Today will be a success if we can get you in the air over the parking lot. But I wanted to show you this still. This is the spot where I hope you'll fly one day. Not today, but soon."

"Wow. Let's try and focus on today. Maybe this bird doesn't have wings after all."

"Hey! Dad! Come over here and see what the professor has built for you!" Thomas was back awake and as excited as ever.

Cody wheeled himself back to where the cars were parked. The trunk of the Volkswagen was open now, showing off what the professor had brought along.

The wings themselves were at least six feet long each. Cody assumed the frame was made of lightweight, aircraft-grade aluminum that was much stronger than it appeared to be when you held it.

The wings themselves were made of dark green nylon fabric pulled tight and stitched around the frames. They looked exactly like the wings of a bat, the only flying mammal out there to lead by example.

In the center of the two wings, there was a harness connected to what looked like a back brace, sized exactly to Cody's body.

It was obvious where Cody's body went, where his arms connected to the wings, and how the contraption worked. For something that sounded so complex, the design was shockingly simple.

"What do you think?"

Cody smiled. "I don't know. Thomas, what do you think?"

"Dad! THIS IS THE COOLEST THING IN THE WORLD! I can't believe you're going to fly with this! You're like a superhuman!"

"Well, Professor. It seems like the consensus is in, and it should work pretty well for us here. When do we get started?"

"What's the point in waiting? Let's get started. Ryan, give me a hand here. Let's get this up and going. Thomas, you grab that skateboard setup and follow us up that hill."

The five of them headed up the hill, Ryan and Professor Reilley with the wings, Thomas rolling two skateboards attached side-by-side, and Sally pushing Cody.

It wasn't a smooth journey. The wheelchair struggled on the bits of gravel spread out along the path, Ryan and the professor dropped the wings at least twice, and Thomas ran up and down the hill a total of ten times to get the skateboards each time they made an escape.

Once they had gotten up to the top, they discussed the plan moving forward. Professor Reilley showed Cody how to get in and out of the contraption by himself using built-in pull cords that would lead to a full release.

Cody strapped himself in and got a feel for moving the wings around with his arms. After months of heavy lifting and an entire life full of movement, they seemed as light as a feather – just as they should.

The plan was this: Cody would strap himself in with Professor Reilley up at the top of the hill. From there, he would be able to gather the momentum he needed to utilize the aerodynamics of the wings to help him take off.

"It's either this or you have to jump off the bluff," the professor had pointed out when Cody showed his first sign of hesitation about the skateboards.

So, he went along with it. The skateboards were set up directly under his torso. When he felt the first pull upwards, he was meant to start slowly moving the wings up and down to get the proper lift.

The wings were designed to provide a large amount of lift without too much flapping necessary. They were like a glider with the built-in option to help you ascend.

Cody was meant to simply circle the parking lot and come back to land in the grassy patch where the professor had laid out an assortment of gymnastic mats and climbing pads that he had borrowed from his school's recreation center.

All the while, Sally was going to be in charge of recording the whole thing, hoping to catch the first human-powered flight on tape.

Ryan was placed as a moving support system. He was essentially tasked with not letting Cody take a turn toward the bluff or crash with too much force. The professor hadn't given him any instructions on how to complete his task but seemed adamant that Ryan would figure it out if the time came.

Thomas was simply in charge of being the leader of all moral support. Everyone started to feel nervous right before the first attempt – save Thomas, of course, who continued running around the parking lot with seemingly endless energy.

It was around 8:30 when the entire team was in place, a little later than originally planned, but Professor Reilley was giddy with excitement and didn't mention it.

"Alright, Prof, are you sure this isn't going to end with me hanging from a tree down over that edge?" Cody asked, pointing out over the massive bluff.

"Cody, how can we be sure of anything in life? Birds don't usually know how to fly on their first attempt. So am I sure? Not at all. But am I hopeful? Now that I can answer with a definitive yes."

The look in the professor's eyes seemed to Cody like those of a man who knew gold was coming up with the next strike of his pickaxe. It wasn't reassuring, to say the very least.

But Cody had worked hard for this, and he had his own degree of hope that he'd worked on building up over the past few months. He sat there now, thinking back on everything that had happened in the past months. He had certainly come a long way from those first days after the accident, and although he was extremely hopeful, part of him knew it would work.

"Alright then. Let's try it out already! I'm all strapped in."

The professor asked Cody one last time. "And what's the process again?"

"We've been over this a hundred times, Prof! I know what I'm doing by now." The professor had gone over the movements with Cody every day in the last week, ensuring that he would know the progression step-by-step when the moment arrived.

"Just one more time, Cody."

"Fine. Keep the wings level. Halfway down the hill, tilt them up at no more than a 15-degree angle. Finally, when I feel lift, start to slowly pump my arms. Just enough to get me up off the skateboard. From there, let the wings do the work. Maybe, if I need to, put one more solid pump in and twist my core in the direction I want to fly. Landing, well, at least we know I won't break my legs," Cody laughed to himself.

"Perfect! Let's go!" He shouted out to Sally, Ryan, and Thomas, who were down in position for the flight. "Everyone, take your marks! This is the first attempt at flight. Taking off in…FIVE!"

Cody's dad flashed through his mind, the two of them building the tree fort together.

"FOUR!"

He saw the cub that he had brought home, remembering feeling its warmth as he bottle-fed it all winter long.

"THREE!"

Then there was his wedding day. Sally, standing at the end of the aisle, everyone he loved all gathered around.

"TWO!"

A collage of brief memories of Thomas running around the house, starting to show his own personality, flooded Cody's mind.

"ONE!"

Then it was his accident, that initial feeling of seeing his legs completely gone from his body. Learning that he would never ride again.

"HERE WE GO!"

The professor put his whole body into pushing Cody toward the edge of the hill.

Cody shook himself out of his daydreaming and back to Mora Point. All of a sudden, he was rushing down the hill, already feeling the airflow pulling hard on his wings.

The power of it all was so much more than he expected. Keeping his arms level was nearly impossible, so he let his arms angle upwards slightly, hoping it would be easier.

Any attempt at pumping his arms downward was completely beaten down by the sheer force of the air in the wings. All of

Cody's energy was going into keeping his arms and body steady, and there wasn't a drop left to spare.

Then he was at the bottom of the hill, racing directly at the tree that called the parking lot home. He only had time to think about the irony of being a downhill mountain biker his entire life and finding himself unable to go down this tiny hill without calamity.

Then he crashed.

Sally dropped her phone and ran to him while the professor came barreling down the hill. Ryan swooped Thomas up on his way over.

When Sally got to Cody, the wings were bent, and his arms were still attached. She reached up and unclipped his arms, which fell limply down to his sides.

Cody was breathing, and Sally could hear what sounded like muffled whimpering. His face was buried in his own shoulder against the tree.

He turned and looked up at her, face covered in blood and mud.

He was laughing.

Sally hadn't seen a grin of this size on Cody's face since before the accident.

He was actually laughing.

"Oh, BOY! Was that good, or was that GOOD?" Cody kept laughing and brought Thomas into his arms right as Ryan came over with him.

"Did you see that, buddy? That was incredible! Boy, I haven't felt a rush like that since I was your age!"

"Dad, aren't you hurt? You're bleeding! Are you missing a tooth? It looks like you might be missing a tooth."

Cody just kept laughing. "Who needs teeth when you're about to fly?"

"What do you mean, dad? You hit this tree; you didn't fly."

Kids. Always with the obvious, and always brutally honest.

"That's right. I hit this tree! But you know what I know now? I know that I can do it. I was so close. I feel so – alive!"

Sally looked a bit worried, but Ryan was laughing along with Cody, and he attempted to reassure her.

"This is barely a crash, Sal. He's had worse than this during our training rides just to get back up and go do something crazier."

He was right. Cody had always been prone to crashing, but always bounced right back up no matter what happened. It seemed like that was what he wanted to do this time too.

"Can I get up there and get at it again, Prof? Now that I know how much force it actually puts on me, I think I can get it done."

"Well, as much as I want to see you get up in the air today, Cody, take a look at your left wing."

Cody looked over past his left arm. A few feet into the wing, the frame had bent ninety degrees, looking like a bat that had a really bad day.

He was disappointed; that much was obvious. But he tried not to let it show too much.

"Alright. Dang. Well, I guess I'm going to need to get straight back to the gym then. I think I have a grasp on the workouts I need to focus on. Plus, I imagine I can still lose a couple of pounds if I really try. That should make it so much easier."

The professor pointed out what everyone else was thinking. "Careful, Cody. You can't afford to lose much more weight. I know it'll be easier, but you need to retain all of the muscle you have now. And you're only muscle at this point."

"Well, how long is it going to take to get that wing back up and running? Like I said, I'm ready to go again today!"

"It'll definitely be a bit longer than today. Take the week to recuperate from your new injuries, and we can probably try again next weekend. I have an idea to reinforce the wings while making them a bit lighter as well."

"I guess that's how it's going to be then. A week from today. We'll be here."

Sally helped Cody get cleaned up with baby wipes from the trunk of their car while Ryan helped disassemble the wings and put them back in the professor's van.

By the time they had wrangled Thomas back in from running around and climbing trees, it wasn't even noon.

They stopped at a small diner on the way home, where everyone but Cody got milkshakes to celebrate the first attempt. Cody, still watching his weight, settled for a salad. The whole time he could only restate how great he felt when going down that hill.

He pushed them to get home as soon as possible so he could get back to training and prepare himself for the next flight.

CHAPTER TEN

A week after Cody's first failed attempt, he found himself back on top of the hill at Mora Point. However, this time, the hill seemed smaller and more manageable, but maybe that was just how Cody chose to see it.

He had spent every moment since the demoralizing failed flight working toward making this one successful. The gym became his first home; he only came back to Sally and Thomas after he could hardly move.

His first attempt had shown him what he needed to work on. The movement and stabilization of his arms had felt so awkward, but that was only because he had focused on the wrong muscle groups. Now it made so much more sense, and Cody worked closely with Ryan to fine-tune their workout routine to fit reality.

The week went exactly like that, with Cody and Ryan in the gym, Cody coming home late, and Sally and Thomas starting to miss him. Thomas kept his excitement about his dad being the first flying man, but Sally started to become unsure.

She had a stronger sense of worry since the first crash. He'd made it out unscathed, but how could she be sure it would always end happily? Any time she brought this worry up with Cody, he dismissed it entirely, saying he'd already had his life's biggest crash. Lightning only struck in the same place once, right?

She decided to suck it up and deal with her worries alone rather than continue to bother Cody. He was dead set on making this next flight his first success.

When the time finally came, they all drove up together, just like the previous week. This time, the car ride was a bit more solemn, lacking the jokes the first ride had been filled with. Everyone's nerves were a bit higher this time.

From the last attempt, they all knew the routine. When they pulled up, Thomas ran straight to Professor Reilley's van, wanting to see the new updates he had put on the wings.

The professor was happy to show off his new designs, explaining to Thomas that he used two new lateral braces that acted like a sixth support system.

"So, this is like how bats' fingers are like ours but stretched out along their wings?" Thomas asked, happy to show off his newfound learning.

"Exactly! But this time, I've added a sixth rod and slightly reduced the diameter of the other support rods to cut down on weight. The extra strength of the sixth rod will more than make up for the lost strength of moving to a smaller rod. It's truly brilliant, if you ask me."

"Whoa! One day, I'm going to build flying machines too. I hope it's okay that I use all of your great ideas!" Thomas bolted off to tell his mom and dad all about the new design.

The professor followed slowly behind him and started to rattle off the daily weather reports before even greeting the McCullys.

"Sunny, all day long! There shouldn't be a single breeze in the sky. If there ever was a day for you to fly, this is the one." His excitement was clear, and the higher energy was needed for the others after a long and quiet car ride.

The good news about the weather seemed to jostle Cody back to life. "That's great! I think this is the one, Prof. I'm feeling great today, and all of the new exercises we added into the routine are going to completely change the way I can hold myself up with the wings."

"Well, then there's no need to stand around talking about it, is there? Let's get going! Ryan, will you help me haul the wings back up to the top of the hill?"

Ryan simply nodded, sharing a bit of the nervous energy that Sally was carrying with her. It was his job to spot Cody and make sure he didn't dive-bomb off the cliff, after all.

While the professor and Ryan grabbed the newly designed wings and started bringing them up the hill, Sally pushed Cody up behind them.

She had tried so hard to keep her nerves under control, but it was bound to happen that she would have to say something.

"Listen, Cody. I know you don't want me to say anything, but I have to."

Cody didn't respond.

"I just – well, I'm just nervous. I don't want Thomas growing up without you like you had to do without your dad around. That's a big cliff, and who knows what would happen if you veered off that way."

Cody still had nothing to say back.

"All I'm saying is, we love you. I've always loved you. I don't think I can stand to be without you. So be careful, alright?"

This time, Cody turned his head and gestured for Sally to stop pushing.

"Sal. I love you more than you may ever know. But this is important to me. I can't get through life without trying to do something, and this is what's in front of me right now, so I'm going to take the chance. I'm going to fly. I promise I'll do it as safely as possible, but we both know that life comes with its risks, and avoiding those only takes away your freedom."

Cody paused before adding in a final thought.

"Isn't that what we want to teach Thomas? Life's worth living, not avoiding. That's why I love you, because I know you believe in that, and you believe in me. So, let's go show our boy what living can be."

Sally smiled, holding back tears as she leaned down to give Cody a quick kiss on the cheek, then started pushing him forward with more of a purpose behind her.

Cody found himself back at the top of the hill. Maybe it was the pep talk he had just given Sally, or maybe it was the extra confidence from his last week of pure physical work, but he knew that success was coming along.

The wings felt more comfortable this time when he strapped in. The professor had adjusted the straps to sit a bit higher on Cody's arm, allowing for more movement in the elbow.

He explained that this should add to Cody's range of motion, expanding the muscle groups that he would engage while working to fly, rather than being totally restricted to one area.

It made sense to Cody, not that he felt like he needed any extra help at this point.

Then the time came for Cody to get out of his chair and onto the skateboard contraption, which was only a bit scratched and beat up from carrying Cody down the hill and barreling into a tree along with him on the last go.

By the time Cody was fully ready to go, Ryan, Thomas, and Sally had made their way to the bottom of the hill and taken up a few positions. Sally had strapped an old sleeping pad to the tree Cody ran into last time, just in case things weren't any different on this go-round.

The presence of the sleeping pad and the reminder that he had crashed only fed Cody's fire and drive to make this time work.

Just like that, it was time to fly.

Cody set himself up and gave the wings a few test flaps, moving them up and down to get a good feel for them.

They felt lighter this time, but it also felt more natural, kind of like he was made for the wings. They had become more a part of him since the last time.

He gave Professor Reilley the go-ahead to move him toward the slope.

Gravity took over quickly, and the lack of wind allowed for him to gain speed more quickly this time around. About a third of the way down the hill, he could start to feel the wings pulling up on him, and his arms fought to keep the wings angled the right way for the wind to catch him.

Halfway down the hill, he was barely touching the skateboard anymore. He could feel it come and go as he was carried up and down with the wings.

With one strenuous push, he was able to bring the wings down and propel himself off the skateboard just enough that it rolled out from under him and shot straight into the bush to the left of Sally.

Now, with the skateboard gone, he had nothing holding him up from the ground, but he was still moving.

He was flying.

His entire body radiated with joy as this realization hit him. He was actually doing it. Now that he was off the ground, the entire process felt worth all of the work he had put into it, worth getting rid of his legs entirely.

Even as his mind raced with thoughts of celebration and joy, he still had to fight to keep himself up and moving. He sloppily steered himself around to the left and away from the bluff, but the open field nearby was still all the way across the paved parking lot. No falling there, he decided.

He put all of his strength into moving his wings and bringing himself upward. There wasn't a single exercise he had done in the gym that could match the brute strength it took to flap his wings and fly through the sky.

Yet he managed to move them and keep up in the air.

Eventually, he completely passed over the parking lot and found himself above the open field, allowing him to relax a bit. Everyone was running underneath him, shouting up at him.

He couldn't hear a single word anyone was saying. He briefly hoped it wasn't a shout of warning; if it was, it was drowned out by the wind coursing through his wings and ears.

He didn't even care about the potential of falling at this point. He felt better than he ever had, knowing all of his work had finally paid off. He allowed himself to quickly think about how his dad would have reacted to seeing him flying over this field, legless and all.

His excitement couldn't last too much longer as his arms started to completely give out, and he couldn't sustain much more time in the air. As of now, he was fully coasting; there was no way his arms could muster the strength to bring himself any higher.

He started to slowly lose height as he circled the field. From the 75 or 80 feet he was at, it only took about a half minute for him to need to prepare for landing – which he hadn't even thought about.

As he raced toward the ground, seemingly heading for another crash, he thought to throw every last muscle in his body into bringing his core and tilting the wings upward to act as a braking system of sorts.

Surprisingly enough, it kind of worked.

He hit the ground, still cruising at a steady speed, but the crash was much more controlled than the last time.

Everyone came charging at him, screaming in excitement.

Thomas was the first one there, jumping straight into his dad's arms without even thinking that he might be hurting. Cody was able to wrap his wings around Thomas, thinking back on his in-flight thoughts about his own dad. He held him like that tightly until the others reached them.

"Cody! That was INCREDIBLE!" Ryan's face was completely lit up. Cody hadn't seen him looking this happy since his wedding day.

Sally ran up and gave Cody an intense hug before finally rolling back onto the grass and helping Cody get free of his wings.

The professor simply asked Cody how it had gone.

"It was amazing, Prof. I've never felt that free before. I didn't really know what was going on, I just listened to my body, and it helped steer me. But man, was it hard to stay up there. It must have been, what? Maybe a minute?"

"Cody, you were up there for 3 minutes and 42 seconds." The professor tossed him a stopwatch that Cody hadn't even seen him pull out at the beginning.

"Almost four minutes? That's insane! It felt like no time at all, but also almost like forever. I don't know how to explain it. It all just felt so worth it. All of the struggles. Everything I've put toward it."

Thomas jumped back in, shoving a phone in his dad's face. "Look! Look at yourself flying, Dad! It's so cool! You look like a giant bat. One of those flying fox bats mom showed me, but bigger!"

Cody watched the video, still struggling to believe it was him that the camera captured. The man in the video looked so calm, so calculated.

He hadn't felt that. Yes, he was excited and happy, but all of that energy had been radiating off him in what he figured looked like frantic chaos, not the calm demeanor he showed in the video.

"Cody, this is perfect! Now we have to talk about making this public! Think about the reporters and all the news outlets. They're going to eat this up. You're going to be famous. We're going to be famous!"

Professor Reilley started to go further down the rabbit hole about making a public appearance and all of the new things they would be able to do with the money and help from others.

"Whoa, whoa, whoa. I know you're excited, Prof. I don't know about the public appearance. Not quite yet. This was my first flight, and it was shaky. I think there's a long way to go before showing anyone else and I'd really appreciate the support in that."

"Well. Yes. I guess I understand. But the season is closing! We need to get you up and flying before the winter hits. Otherwise, we'll totally miss our chance to show the world!"

"But what if I don't *want* to show the world? I don't remember that being a part of the deal."

"Why else would we do this? So you can fly around for fun? No. This was about bringing a new development to the world. Showing everyone that human flight is real and totally possible! We must show them. Otherwise, this is for nothing." The professor was obviously becoming irritated with the hesitancy Cody was showing about a public flight.

Sally jumped in before the tensions could rise any higher than they were already. "Hey now, everyone, take a breather. This was awesome. Let's focus on that. I don't think we need to schedule a press conference quite yet. Don't spoil the moment."

"Yeh, that's right. Let's just enjoy it, right, guys?" Ryan was quick to join in on Sally's calming presence, trying to show his support.

Both Cody and the professor quieted down, but there were still some signs of tension between the two of them.

Cody spoke up first.

"Right. Well, I don't know about the public appearance, but I'm not saying no right now either. I just want to feel more comfortable in these things before showing them off to the world. I can't stand the idea of embarrassing myself and becoming 'Cody No Legs, the man who can't walk or fly.' You know what I mean?"

"Yes. I'm terribly sorry for the way I acted. I think you're right, and we should definitely practice more. Let's see what you can do. Do you feel up for another round today?"

"Prof, I think I could fly all day and never get tired of the feeling of being up there. Let's go for round two."

All five of them stayed out at Mora Point the entire day.

Cody took flight five times that day alone. By the end, he could barely get himself to sit up straight, but he was demonstrating a lot of comfort strapping into the wings by the end of the day.

The professor didn't mention bringing the suit out in public again the rest of the day, likely in great thanks to Sally. She had pulled him aside again before the second flight and encouraged him to just give Cody time.

He had always been nervous about big bike competitions, and this wouldn't be any different. Either way, he always came around and actually enjoyed showing off for the public to some degree.

Because of that, the whole crew had a great time eating, playing, and joking around while watching Cody fly. It became quite a normal day for the first man to take off in fully sustained flight.

CHAPTER ELEVEN

The day arrived, and everything was perfect. The sun beamed down onto the grassy hills surrounding Mora Point, the wind had taken the day off, as there wasn't even a little breeze, and Cody felt better than ever.

In the parking lot, cars were still streaming in. All the way down the road, the vans of local news media outlets were parked halfway on the asphalt, halfway in the ditch. Cody briefly wondered how many people would struggle to get their cars out at the end of the day.

Professor Reilley had spread the word like wildfire over the last few weeks since Cody had taken flight. He teased news outlets with secrets of new developments that everyone would be amazed by. He told fellow scientists about a breakthrough discovery unlike any seen in the last century.

Newspapers and television channels from the surrounding areas sent their journalists out in hoards. There wasn't much certainty about what to expect. The professor had worked hard to sell them enough to get people sent out to cover the story.

What he hadn't done was tell anyone exactly what was going on at Mora Point that day.

As a result, there were heaps of confusion mixed with curiosity. Speculation had gone around about what was happening. Guesses ranged from an extinct species being brought back to this all being a hoax created by a professor who had become seen as wild and out of his mind.

Both the professor and Cody had heard each one of these rumors but had done nothing to stop them. The more the people were guessing, the more surprised they would be when Cody took flight at the base of Mora Point.

Cody and Sally wandered around amongst all the journalists crowding the parking lot as they began to prep for the flight. They'd gotten everything set up early that morning, so there was nothing to do now but wait.

"Wow. I guess the professor has some great connections, huh?" Cody whispered to Sally as they worked their way to the front of the crowd.

"Are you sure you want to do this? Won't they all recognize you from your racing days?"

"Maybe. I think I recognize some of these guys. I imagine the professor used my name to get some of them interested in the first place." Cody shrugged off the pressure that loomed all around him.

Sally looked more worried than Cody felt at that moment.

"All I'm saying is, if you don't want to do this, we can turn and walk away right now."

"I know. And I love you for that. But, Sally, how I feel when I'm flying... It's hard to explain. I haven't felt so...free since I was on my bike. I don't care who's watching; I just want to fly again."

Sally had nothing to say to that, so she settled for grabbing Cody's arm and burying her face into his shoulder before they set off to the top of the hill together.

Once they arrived at the top, Cody turned around and scanned the crowd for Thomas, who, to his disliking, had to stay in the crowd with Ryan.

He spotted them right at the front of the crowd, Thomas looking around nervously and Ryan with his arms around his shoulders. Cody caught Ryan's eye and waved, hoping to ease Thomas's obvious tension just a bit.

When Thomas saw him, he simply turned around and showed him the new cape Sally had helped him put together. It was an old Superman cape, but they had taken one of Cody's old biking jerseys and sewn it over the big "S."

Cody's grin covered his face as he turned around to look for Professor Reilley to go over his flight path for the day one more time. They wanted to make it grand and put on a big show for the media, but they also needed to keep it safe and comfortable for Cody.

In the end, they'd settled on a route that took him out along the bluff's edge and over the trees of the surrounding forest. He would do a few circles around the parking lot and then head toward the open field.

Over the field, he could work on showing off a bit.

He'd flown a few times since the first day and had started to get more control over his movements – tilting his wings, relaxing a muscle, and even engaging his core in different ways all greatly affected how he could fly.

Just like with biking, he'd gotten good – really good.

Once they'd settled on their plan and gone over it again and again, they set about strapping Cody into position between the two wings.

The crowd below stood watching Cody as he got strapped in. There were murmurs passed from person to person, guessing what would happen. For a crowd full of people who had no idea what was happening, it was oddly quiet.

From the quiet came the small but mighty voice of Thomas McCully.

"Let's go, Dad!" he screamed at the top of his lungs.

That was when Cody set forward, allowing gravity to take over and bring him coursing down the hill. He had worked with Professor Reilley to add lead weights along the deck of the skateboard, creating more speed on his way down the hill.

In the past training flights, the increased speed had made it easier for Cody to stay in the air even longer with each run.

As he began to speed down the hill, the entire crowd went crazy. The realization was there now. A man was trying to fly.

Cameras went off, and reporters started talking into their microphones, hoping to catch every moment of what was happening and be the first to bring the news home with them.

Cody seamlessly took flight only halfway down the hill and began on his course along the bluff line, earning a few gasps and whoops of excitement.

Once he lifted off the ground, the crowd below faded into the background of his mind. Just like every time he had flown over the last month, the feeling of being up in the air drowned out any other noise inside his head.

This was where he felt free. Up there, Cody had full control. It didn't matter that he had lost his old life as a mountain biker. It didn't matter that he'd lost his dad so many years ago.

His life completely shifted to the present moment when he was flying. The past was left behind on the ground, sitting amongst the reporters. His future was right ahead of him, and he knew that it only held more flying.

Moving through the sky was like a dance. It felt like it had years ago when he would fly down the racetrack on his bike. Each turn was planned with precision and executed with perfection.

Unlike biking, he could play more in the air. There were no obstacles to avoid, and all he needed to do was focus on flying. But Cody had always been one to show off just a little bit.

He danced to the left and the right, moving his body in a way that few, if any, had before.

He edged himself out over the bluff, where only 1,000 feet of nothingness stood between him and the ground. The risk wasn't even apparent to Cody; he still could only feel the bliss of being in flight.

Following the planned course, Cody brought himself back over the parking lot and the trees surrounding it. He dipped down into the trees, narrowly avoiding some as he sped past them. Pushing his arms to their breaking point, he could bring himself in and out of the forest, providing a constant level of suspense for the onlooking crowd.

Twisting his body and adjusting his wings allowed him to curve sharply toward the field, where he planned on landing, but not just yet.

At this point, Cody had been in sustained flight for around fifteen minutes, and his body could feel the exhaustion setting in.

Previously, he'd only been able to stay up for thirteen minutes, but today he had set his sights on making it to the twenty-minute mark. After a quick glance at his watch, he began to doubt that it would be possible.

To keep himself in flight even longer, he avoided the planned tricks he'd been working on over the field. They took a lot of power out of him, and he didn't have any power to give up at this point.

Instead, Cody settled on simply gliding and enjoying being up in the air for the few minutes of strength he had left in him. He didn't want to think about having to touch back down on the ground where everyone stood waiting for him.

The reporters had moved from the parking lot down the road to the open field where they had set their cameras back up, likely hoping for some dramatic crash when Cody tried to land.

The professor and Sally were out in front of them, laying down a runway made of old gym mats and blankets to soften the landing.

Up until today, the previous landings had all been pretty rough. Cody couldn't get much control over his landing, so he often settled for a graceful crash rather than slowing himself down too much.

As he came in for the landing this time, Sally noticed him bring his hips forward and tilt his head and arms backward, allowing the wings to catch more air and hopefully slow his landing down.

It seemed like the motion slowed him down some, but not nearly enough.

Cody crashed into the pads. Collapsing in sheer exhaustion, he allowed the wings to fall to the ground beside him.

The crowd of reporters rushed to form a tight circle around him, barely giving him any space to recover from his crash landing.

Sally was obviously upset with the way that the crowd rushed him, shouting for them to back up and let them get Cody up and out of the device.

Surprisingly, the crowd listened and stayed quiet while Sally and the professor unlatched the straps that held Cody in place and got him over and into his wheelchair.

Once he was settled in, Professor Reilley pulled out a small microphone with speakers so Cody could talk to the audience before leaving for home and some well-deserved rest.

"I guess I don't really know what to say," Cody managed to get out, still working on catching his breath.

"I've been flying now for about a month. And what I can tell you is, there's nothing in this world more freeing than taking off into the skies. It doesn't matter that I don't have my legs anymore. When I fly, I'm finally free again."

The crowd waited for Cody to say more. When he didn't, the questions exploded from each and every journalist out there.

One reporter managed to bring his voice to the forefront, forcing his question to be heard.

"Why do it? Why put your life at such risk?" He asked.

Thomas had appeared by Cody's side. Putting his arms around his son, Cody replied, "I don't think about it like that. I think sitting at home, spending every day in this chair, and showing my son that I've admitted defeat is putting my life at risk.

"Flying, on the other hand – flying is taking the chance to actually live. I want to show my son, and the world, that life shouldn't be feared, and no one should sit back and watch as it all disappears in a flash."

Another reporter jumped in as soon as Cody stopped talking.

"What are your plans for the future? Do you think you'll be able to keep in the air even longer?"

Cody laughed, having just thought about his past, present, and future while in the air.

"For now, flying is my future. Today I set my own personal record of eighteen and a half minutes in the air, but I know I'm capable of much more."

A third journalist hopped in and asked, "How are you going to do it? I'm under the impression it took you ages to get to this point."

"That's a great question. And to be honest, I don't really know. But I imagine I'm going to hit the gym and train harder than I have before. Plus, now I can spend more time flying and getting used to it. I'm working on going from a flying turkey to a hawk, so there's a lot to be done."

With that, Cody said his thanks to everyone that showed up and handed the microphone over to Professor Reilley.

"Everyone, thank you for coming! As you've all seen here today, we have gotten the first human up in the air with fully self-sustained flight. The only goal is to fly further forward from here. I can take two more questions before we start packing up our gear."

A female reporter stepped forward with a microphone and asked, "Hi, Cynthia Shaw with the Herald Gazette. Professor, where exactly did this idea even come from? You're a biologist at the university, correct? So why modify a human this way when we can already hop on an airplane?"

Without hesitation, the professor replied, "Cynthia. I've been dreaming of flying ever since I was a small child. I watched the birds in my backyard as they took flight, making the life below them look so irrelevant. Unfortunately, my past lineage hasn't given me the most athletic of bodies, so it needed to be someone else. Human beings are capable of so much more than we allow ourselves to achieve."

He paused and looked over at Cody. "When life takes us down, there's an opportunity to get back up and rise above where we once were. Cody is showing the world that it is possible."

The crowd was quiet, a few heads nodding in response as if they fully understood the message the professor was trying to convey.

The first reporter was the first to break the silence. "And when will we get to see what exactly Cody is capable of next?"

"Well, I'll have to talk to Cody about that. But with the weather starting to go against us, there's a shorter period of time left than we would like. I believe we will need to fly within the next month to make the weather window we'd like. The next flight will be bigger, and we are hoping to come up with the location in the next week or so to announce the upcoming flight."

The professor said thank you and ignored the remaining questions being shouted at him.

Ryan and the professor worked to get the contraption loaded up in the professor's van while the reporters packed up their own gear and drove off.

Soon, the parking lot was completely empty, leaving the McCully family, Ryan, and the professor to sit in silence for the first time all day.

It was the first time that Ryan could even talk with Cody since the flight, and he wanted to know everything. "How did it feel this time? You crushed your record, and you looked super solid up there. I didn't think you'd come down."

Cody smiled. "Yeh, it was awesome. I think all the pressure brought me back to our biking days. Performing best under pressure has always been my M.O."

"We've got at least one more flight to pressure you into. Hopefully, this time, it can push you even further to maybe thirty minutes."

"Thirty minutes, I can do. I know it. I just need to fly more. The gym isn't going to give me what I need. I'll look for a small local field that I can try out."

Thomas perked up. "Dad! What about that hill above my little league field? That's pretty steep, and you can fly around the field whenever there's not a game going on."

"I think that's a great idea, little man. Prof, can we get that rig into our car? Promise I'll take good care of it."

The professor winced. "You've already wrecked this thing once or twice. I'll agree to it, but only if Ryan and Sally are there to make sure you don't break the wings – or yourself."

"Well, Professor. You've got yourself a deal. Let's get everything moved over. We've got some flying to do."

CHAPTER TWELVE

"Throw another 40 pounds on there, Ryan."

Cody was laying down on the bench, going on his fifth straight hour at the gym that day. Ever since his big first public flight, he'd barely left the gym.

"Are you sure? We're pushing your max, and I don't think you want to get hurt before the next flight."

Ryan had played the part of Cody's lifting buddy but also his safety net during these long gym days. Cody wanted to push himself, often far past his limits.

In Ryan's head, he was asking to get hurt.

"Just throw it on; I'll only go for a few reps," Cody snapped before shuffling himself back into position.

Ryan went ahead and loaded up the bar for Cody. The gym sessions had gone this way consistently over the last few weeks. The more Cody trained, the unhappier he began to seem.

Each time Ryan brought it up, Cody shrugged it off and told him he was fine. Regardless, it kept coming up over and over again.

Cody adjusted his hands on the bar, preparing for a massive bench press that was just below his maximum weight.

He lifted it up off the rests and brought it slowly down to his chest. As soon as he started to press up, Ryan could tell it wasn't going to happen.

He grabbed the bar and gave the extra support necessary for Cody to get the bar back onto the rests.

"Damn it! This is nothing! I should be able to lift this. If only the professor would allow me to eat real food for once in my life. I'm sick and tired of protein shakes and mixed greens. Remember when we used to go and load ourselves up with burgers at Heidi's?"

It was often about the food that he was not allowed to eat. Ryan understood that. He'd been Cody's friend for his entire life and was well aware of how much the man could eat.

"Hey, we'll be back at Heidi's before you know it. You just have to get through this one flight, and then the season is totally over. It'll be time to take a break."

Ryan had no idea how much of a break Cody would actually get to take, but he tried to reassure his friend that there was some level of freedom coming his way.

The two of them worked together to get Cody moved from the bench into his wheelchair so they could head home for the day. At this point, Cody often got quiet, not wanting to give up for the day but needing to listen to his body.

Most of the time, Ryan would just take Cody home and head home himself. Cody would sit at home with Sally and Thomas, eat dinner, sleep early, and get up to do it all again. Cody was stuck in this repetition of working out, eating, and sleeping, and Ryan figured he needed a break.

"How about we head over to Heidi's and take a break from the strict diet and routine of it all?" Ryan suggested as he glanced over at Cody.

Cody looked torn between the choice of his strict routine and finally letting himself relax a bit.

"I don't know, Ryan. The next flight is only a week out. I don't think I can let myself go yet."

"Cody, man. You're miserable. I've barely seen you smile in the last month. You have to let yourself breathe a bit."

"But that's the thing. I'm not happy because I'm not in the air right now. When I'm up there, it's the best feeling I can imagine. It's the only time I've felt free since the accident. This training allows me to keep flying and feeling free. I can't just sacrifice that for a few cheeseburgers."

Ryan hesitated. He wanted to support Cody and help him find happiness, but from his perspective, it didn't seem to be happening.

"Your life can't be reduced to the time you're up in the air. How can we find a way for you to feel free without destroying yourself just to get in the air?"

Cody wheeled himself over to the exit without a response. He knew he needed to find happiness, but getting up in the air and out of his chair had been the only way to find it.

The ride home was completely silent. The two of them hardly ever felt disconnected in this way. Their friendship had its fair share of small disputes, but this one felt different. Cody seemed different. He had always been the optimistic one that pushed Ryan to be better and try harder. It was Ryan's turn to step up and try to get Cody back to his regular self.

When he dropped Cody off at home, Ryan hung back to talk with Sally. He knew he needed to work toward helping Cody out, but he also knew he couldn't do it alone.

She came over to the car window as Cody wheeled himself into the living room to hang out with Thomas before he hit the sack.

"How's he been at home? Every time we're at the gym, he talks about how unhappy he is and how badly he wants to get back into the air. I'm starting to worry that this whole flying thing is actually bad for him."

Sally slowly nodded her head in agreement.

"At home, he's just about the same. I mean, he puts on a strong face for Thomas, but other than that, we never laugh like we used to. We never get the chance to play together or really have any fun. It's all about the next flight."

The two of them were quiet for a moment, in solidarity during the rough times faced together.

Ryan was the first to speak. "The flying itself probably isn't bad for him. It's just that it's taken over every moment, every aspect, of his entire life."

"What about getting out to one of those old forest service cabins this weekend? We can all spend some time together, Cody can find some time to work out, but we won't let it be the entire day. He used to love getting out there for long weekends."

While it might be a hard sell for Cody, they both knew it would do wonders for the whole family's morale. Even Thomas was starting to see through the cracks and read into what was really going on with his dad.

The weekend retreats to the cabin had been a staple of their lives together before the accident. Ryan and Cody would ride their bikes, and Sally, Thomas, and Ryan's ex-girlfriend would always spend their days lounging in the sun or taking turns going out on their bikes.

None of their bodies had gotten enough sunshine in the past few weeks, and with the temperatures already starting to drop as autumn began to settle in, the vitamin D would do wonders for everyone.

In bed that night, Sally proposed the idea to Cody. To her surprise, he was eager to get out to the cabin and spend a weekend with just his family and Ryan.

"Thomas is going to love it. We can bring out that old ramp I built for him last year and set it up in the woods. I can coach him a bit on his jumps. It'll help to be fully present and away from the gym."

Sally could see his face softening and lighting up with the idea of trying out an old family favorite, even amongst the chaos of all the media and plans for the next big flight.

That little part of Cody was still there, and she couldn't be happier to see it poking its head out with the possibility of some sunshine in the future.

The cabin they chose for that weekend was a small little log cabin built by Cody's dad and other volunteers in the early 1970s.

As they pulled up, Thomas jumped out of the car and ran around the cabin to check out every nook and cranny before anyone else could even set foot outside the car.

He sprinted past the towering spruce trees that hadn't changed a bit since Cody's last visit when he was around the same age as Thomas. Then he made his way around the back of the cabin, oblivious to the small signs of his dad's childhood times there.

There were small notches in the trees where Cody had built elaborate forts in the woods, clotheslines spanning the distance between other trees where the family had done their laundry, and even Cody's tiny handprints imprinted in the concrete of the patio his dad had poured during one of their weekend trips.

As the door opened to the car, the memories of his time there flooded Cody's mind. It was a mixture of sadness and nostalgia that confused him even more than thinking about his accident.

It was at that moment that he committed this weekend to helping Thomas form those memories for himself. He wanted this time at the cabin to be about family and having fun together, not about his need to escape the chair and feel alive again.

Ryan's words had really sat with him over the past few days. He wanted to find a way to be happy without relying on the gym and flying.

So he had decided not to even work out that weekend, to go back to being carefree and letting himself indulge in the small pleasures of life.

He let Ryan and Sally help him out of the car and into his wheelchair, which they had retrofitted with old mountain bike tires so he could move easily around the dirt tracks surrounding the cabin.

Then he called over to Thomas to come along with him to test out the new setup on some of the small trails he could remember from when he was younger.

As Ryan and Sally unloaded the car, Cody and Thomas set off into the woods. The two of them raced down the trails, only stopping when there was something exciting that one of them wanted to point out to the other.

Cody came alive again almost immediately. The smell of the pine and spruce trees brought him back to a time when he was happier, without a care in the world.

They found an old rope swing that Cody remembered tying an old tire to with his dad one day.

He had found the tire rotting in the woods near an old fire road and had immediately expressed his sadness to his dad about people leaving their trash around the forest.

His dad had a solution right away. He grabbed an old rope from the small shed behind the cabin and scaled up a tree with the same ease Cody would find later in life. He tied the rope onto an overhanging branch and tossed it down to where Cody waited on the ground.

They worked together to get the tire on the rope and then spent the rest of the day swinging. The only break they took was to get Cody's mom so she could see what they made and come swing with them.

His entire childhood had been full of moments like that one. His dad had inspired him to become such a good father himself, but he felt that part of him slipping away.

Cody snapped out of his memory and back to reality, where Thomas was swinging around on the tire swing.

He shook his head and tried clearing those thoughts so he could focus on helping Thomas swing higher on the tire swing.

Then the rope snapped.

Thomas went tumbling forward and smacked straight into a fallen tree that hadn't even softened up with rot.

Cody heard a crunch and looked on as his son began to scream in pain.

He didn't know what to do. He wheeled over to Thomas but could barely reach him to try and help him up and take him back to the cabin for help. It was at this point that Cody fell out of his wheelchair and landed sprawled out next to Thomas.

Thomas just lay on the ground, writhing in pain, cradling what must have been his fractured arm.

The pain and the injury snatched Cody from where he sat and took him right back to the moment of the bear attack.

He was no longer with Thomas; he was on the ground as the bear clawed at his back. He was back to fighting for his life.

The bear swung at his head and neck, attempting to kill him.

Cody tried to fight the pain and bring himself out of this dream, but he couldn't move underneath the massive weight of the bear, pinning him to the ground.

Just when he didn't think he would be able to get free of the bear, he heard Ryan's voice shouting his name.

"Cody! Cody! What are you doing, man? Get up! We have to get Thomas back over to the cabin!"

Cody broke free from the bear and woke in a cold sweat. Ryan and Sally had run to him when they heard the sound of Thomas screaming from the woods.

They lifted Cody up and into his wheelchair, but he was still completely unable to make any kind of coherent sentence explaining what had happened.

Sally pushed him back to the car and helped load him into the back seat as Ryan carried Thomas over his shoulder and strapped him into the seat next to his dad.

The car peeled out of the dirt driveway and raced toward the same hospital that Cody had woken up in almost a year before.

By the time they got to the hospital, Cody had come to and was able to explain what had happened in the woods. The old rope must have been chewed on by some rodent and then simply given way when Thomas swung too high.

He blamed himself, even after getting the primary report from the doctor explaining that Thomas likely had a compound fracture in his radius, though he needed to examine the X-rays for a definitive diagnosis.

The three of them sat in the waiting room as Thomas was taken into the pediatric radiology section of the hospital. No one really wanted to talk about what happened, and eventually, Ryan said he should probably head home and let them talk about it as a family.

They said their thanks and goodnights, and Ryan went off to call a car to pick him up.

That left Cody and Sally alone in the waiting room, the buzz of the fluorescent lights the only sound in the sterile, empty hospital.

They didn't talk about it much that night, but Cody knew they would need to address what happened at some point. Ever since he got in the chair, he had been feeling like a failure, unable to help his family.

This only made him feel like even more of a failure.

He reflected back on the way he had felt out at the cabin. He had actually believed he could return to normal. He had hoped there was a way out of feeling trapped in his chair.

That turned out to be a mistake. That attempt only left him with the pain of letting his son get hurt.

Flying was the only thing that could help him free himself from the confines of his chair. He wouldn't make the mistake of believing otherwise again.

CHAPTER THIRTEEN

For days, all Cody could do was go back to the gym and come home to a quiet house. Thomas's energy had been back up since the accident, but Cody still hadn't come close to forgiving himself.

Even with Sally, things were off. They had talked about what happened, but Cody still felt the need to hold back how he truly felt. His depression was back, and the only thing he thought about was the next flight.

Things went on at home and at the gym with the big flight day rapidly approaching.

The plan was to have all of the news outlets and researchers from the entire state there, and Professor Reilley claimed that he had some nationwide reporters attending as well.

The pressure only fueled Cody forward. He had come up with his own flight path, designed to truly stun everyone that showed up for the big flight, but had yet to pass it by the professor as it was risky, and some would say crazy.

Although the plan was risky, he thought it would be necessary to redeem himself for what he had done with Thomas. He amped up his training and continued to strive for perfection, not allowing for any slip-ups.

When the big day arrived, he felt as ready as ever. All of his training had gone according to plan, even if things at home were a bit rocky.

The group was heading back up to Mora Point for the big show. It was a familiar spot, and they had trained extensively there. The professor knew the weather patterns by heart, and he was able to predict any slight gust coming up off the river down below.

When they arrived, Cody pulled Professor Reilley to the side to talk to him about his flight plan.

"Prof, I want to take a big risk. I've been thinking a lot, and to get the attention we need, I have to really make a big show this time."

The professor looked dubious. "So what exactly are you thinking? We've had this flight path planned out for weeks. I think it would be best to stick to what we know."

"Yeh, well, I think that it would be better if I fly myself over the edge of the bluff. I can get down on the same level as everyone, so they aren't looking straight up," Cody said.

Shock spread across the professor's face. "Are you mad? I know things have been tough at home recently, but isn't this a bit extreme? You make one false move, and there's nothing but a thousand feet of empty space below you."

"I know, and I've thought about this a lot, but I just don't think I can get the same reaction by doing circles around the old soccer field again. I need something fresh and new. This will get everyone's attention, and isn't that what you want?"

Professor Reilley sat and thought for a moment without a word.

"This is going to work, Prof. I know how people react to these big showy moments. It's all I did in my biking career, and that took me to the top. Trust me on this one."

After another moment of hesitation, the professor agreed to Cody's wild plan. He told him that he needed to talk to Sally about it and have her on board so that he wouldn't be fully at fault.

Cody knew exactly how Sally would react to the plan, so he asked the professor to let him handle that and kept it entirely to himself. He would fly out over the bluff and above the river. There, he would only stick around for a few minutes before making his way back, but he thought that should be enough to wow the crowds.

They set up just like they had for the first televised flight. This time, however, they all came early, expecting a huge crowd to be gathering already. The crowd was massive an hour before the scheduled start of the flight, with barely any space to move Cody through the crowd in his wheelchair.

When Cody reached the top of the hill, he turned and caught sight of Thomas, one arm in a cast, the other making drastic motions while talking to a girl about his age. He had mentioned having a crush on a girl in class, but Cody had been so preoccupied that he hadn't fully registered how crazy that was.

Nonetheless, there he was, dazzling his classmate with the huge personality that Cody loved so much about him. It was entertaining to watch, and it made Cody feel incredibly happy to see his son smiling so much.

This flight was meant to be for Thomas, but Cody knew it was about himself as well. He wanted to prove to himself what he could do while showing off to his son and the crowd. He hoped to make Thomas proud.

The time came, and Ryan helped get Cody strapped into his wing suit while the professor addressed the crowd. He told them about Cody's amazing last flight, and how this time he would be pushing for the thirty-minute mark.

His voice echoed in the back of Cody's mind. He only saw his flight path and could barely hear anything else going on.

When the professor stopped talking and gave the floor to him, Cody didn't even notice Ryan nudging him forward.

Just like that, he was barreling down the hill and taking off into the sky.

People down below started cheering immediately. There was a resounding scream of shock and delight as he tested how he was feeling, swerving to the left and right.

After a few twists and turns in the air, Cody felt confident enough to make his way toward the bluff, earning an even more dramatic response from the crowd.

Just as Cody was about to break the barrier of the bluff, a red-tailed hawk soared past him, only a few feet away from making direct contact with his wings. While the crowd below sounded frightened, Cody was elated.

This was what being alive felt like. This was freedom.

Then he broke out over the bluff line and could see a thousand feet down to the river that curved through the bright orange and yellow trees that were proudly displaying their fall colors.

Cody wanted to keep going further out, but as soon as he turned back toward the bluff, he could see that he'd already flown quite a distance away from the crowd. They were waving their arms back and forth, almost as if they thought him to be lost in the sky.

He surely didn't feel lost; it was as if he'd finally found his place.

Although the temptation was strong, Cody turned himself back toward the crowd and flew in a direct line to the field where he would eventually land.

Just when he was about to reach the bluff line, a strong gust of wind took hold of his wings and veered him sharply off course. For just a moment, Cody felt his stomach drop as he felt out of control for the first time ever in the sky.

He fought the wind, angling his wings back the right way to bring himself back over land, but the current was stronger than he expected. It carried him further and further away from the crowd.

Eventually, he recognized that he could do nothing but go along with it. The breeze seemed to be his guide, so he let it take him and turned around to face away from the crowd.

He picked up speed faster than ever and fought to slow himself, making slow and wide turns like he did when his dad had taken him skiing for the first time almost two decades ago.

That day on the ski hill, he had felt a huge amount of fear. He had stopped, paralyzed, in the middle of the slope. When his dad reached him, he was almost unresponsive. With long and patient guidance, Rex had taken Cody down the hill to the lodge for a hot chocolate.

Today, Rex wasn't around to help Cody down from this hill.

He scanned his surroundings and recognized that the ground was approaching faster than he had imagined. He must have lost altitude quickly in a cold patch of air coming from the river.

Looking around, he could see nothing for miles. He had hoped for a wide open field, but there was nothing but trees.

Then, from behind a grove of trees, he spotted a small dirt road that looked as if it had river access. His in-the-moment decision-making skills from years of racing downhill on his mountain bike took over instantly.

There was no way he was going to reach the road in time, so he chose a wide sandbank on the side of the river that looked as if the landing was somewhat plausible, and less painful than crashing into the trees.

He steered himself toward the sandbank, hoping that he could descend quickly enough to land there rather than on the rocky bed of the river ahead of him.

Almost immediately, he knew that he wasn't going to make the descent quick enough, but he was at a point of no return.

The river past the bank seemed shallow enough to land in without becoming fully submerged, but he couldn't be sure. At this point, all he could do was hope that he was right.

In a flash of cold water, the river engulfed Cody and the entire wingsuit.

The river here was deeper than he had thought; it only looked shallow due to being crystal clear and as cold as ice.

With his mouth, he reached over, fighting the current of the water, and pulled on the emergency release cord for his right arm. It worked as planned, and now he had at least one arm free as the river continued to drag him downstream.

The left release wasn't as helpful. While he yanked on the cord hard, it didn't want to release. He fought and fought the contraption, eventually having to stretch far enough to reach the quick-release pin on his own and maneuver it out of place.

Contorting and stretching his body like this worked, but it also gave him a nose and mouthful of water, making it difficult to breathe.

Cody's mind shot back and forth between the present flow of the river and the feeling of the bear mauling him. The flashbacks made him think to Thomas and what had happened the last time he let his emotions overwhelm him.

He fought hard and brought himself back to this world. He was completely out of energy, but he dug deep to find any last bit of power to pull himself to the shore of the river.

He had been dragged over a hundred yards downstream, but the river had also brought him over to a small tree that looked as if it had fallen into the water recently.

With a single lunge, Cody grabbed hold of the tree as the rest of the wingsuit was torn free from his body by the surging current of the river. A year ago, he never would have been able to hold on to the tree against the power of the water. Having basically lived in the gym, he had become so strong that it was just barely doable.

He crawled hand over hand to the side of the river until the water was shallow enough that the current stopped pulling him. From there, he was able to crawl onto dry land, where he collapsed in exhaustion.

Thirty minutes he had spent in the air. Thirty minutes of flying and overexerting himself, all for some random news channels. The last few minutes in the river were infinitely more tiring than all of his past flights combined.

Cody couldn't muster enough energy to move a muscle, and so he lay there, soaking in the slight relief of the warm sun, hoping that Ryan and Sally would be able to find him.

When he glanced up and down the river, he saw that the wingsuit had been snared by another tree about fifty yards downstream. Hopefully, this would be enough of a marker for everyone to see where he was and come to his rescue.

Then he rested his head against a patch of sand amongst the rocks that he was laying on and closed his eyes.

An hour later, he woke up to Sally shaking him.

"Cody! Cody, are you alright? Cody, wake up!"

Cody opened his eyes and looked up at Sally, also soaking wet and covered in twigs, leaves, and sand. She had fought tooth and nail through the forest and river to get to him.

"Where is everyone?" Cody asked.

"They're coming," Sally reassured him as she lifted his head into her lap. "Just rest for now."

The two of them sat there for another thirty minutes or so. Sally didn't even ask about his stunt of going out over the bluff line. She told him about the immediate response of everyone that had witnessed the flight.

News vans and other spectators had gone straight to their cars and flown down the mountain. Search parties were out in every direction to find him, but she had tried to think about how he would have thought in the air.

She assumed that he would try to find the most wide open space on the river and land there. From above, she had seen a large sandy patch and headed immediately there to start searching up and downstream from that spot. When she saw his wingsuit, she jumped in the river and started swimming toward it until she spotted him on the side of the river.

Fortunately, she had a GPS locator with her that she could send out a message on. The McCully family had always carried them on biking trips in case they got separated.

After a while, there was a rustling in the woods, and Ryan burst out of the trees with an emergency medical team right behind him.

The team loaded him up on a stretcher and carried him to the dirt track that Cody had seen from above. It was only a half mile away from his crash site, but the journey took well over an hour through the thick brush of the forest.

Surprisingly, Cody was completely uninjured. Aside from a few scrapes and rashes, he had escaped any serious injury that would have made him unable to fly again for the rest of the year. It seemed to be a miracle of sorts.

In reality, Cody had just chosen the best possible spot to crash land. Sheer luck.

There was no need for a hospital bed that came with huge fees, so Cody asked to be taken straight home.

After a long ride home, Sally, Ryan, Cody, and Thomas all sat on the couch of their living room.

Cody saw how uncomfortable and scared Thomas looked.

"Thomas, don't start thinking I didn't see you chatting up that classmate of yours," he smiled as Thomas's cheeks went instantly red. "I assume that's the lucky lady that you've been talking about from school?"

Still blushing, Thomas managed a response. "Yeh, that's her. I told her about the flight in class, and she convinced her parents to bring her up to see it! She thought it was so cool!"

Everyone laughed, breaking the tension that had been present since the flight. "Well, I'm glad that I could put on quite the show for her. It was quite the wild ride, wasn't it?"

Ryan clicked on the TV and flipped over to the local news. The first story up was about a small pizza joint that had a family of raccoons drop through the ceiling straight onto a family's pepperoni pie. That story helped everyone lighten up and prepare for the next one.

The reporter on the screen started showing the footage from Cody's flight, warning the audience about the footage that showed him crashing into the river.

Even though Cody considered the flight a total failure, the news outlets weren't reporting it that way at all. They remarked on how incredible his strength was to stay in flight for half an hour, going far beyond what anyone could imagine.

Then they launched into a full bio of Cody, talking about his previous career in mountain biking and covering the incident with the bear, leaving him in a wheelchair.

While they framed Professor Reilley as a bit more of a mad scientist, it was still a fully positive story that praised the immense amount of work that had been put in by everyone involved in the flight.

The story lifted the spirits of the room greatly, almost allowing everyone to forget that Cody had almost lost his life earlier that day.

The family stayed on the couch all night watching the different news channels to see how they reported on Cody. After the second news story, Thomas was completely passed out, asleep on Sally's lap.

A couple hours later, Cody was the only one still awake, watching the stories pass by on the screen. He stayed up late into the night, thinking about flying.

Regardless of the crash, all Cody wanted was to get back up in the air and taste freedom one more time.

CHAPTER FOURTEEN

The phone in the professor's office rang once before he picked it up. On the other end was Cody; Professor Reilley knew that, but all he heard was silence.

It wasn't the first time that Cody had called him and struggled to get his words out, so the professor was patient and simply waited.

After a long moment, he finally started talking.

"Prof, listen. Don't get me wrong here, because I never want to stop flying. But I need a break. I need some time to be up there without the business of the cameras and all the cheering down below," Cody started.

The professor just waited for more, and Cody continued.

"I want to do a flight that's only me. You can come, obviously, and help set everything up, but I want to feel free from everything, and that includes the people that come to watch me like I'm some sort of zoo animal."

He had expressed his concern with being on display more than once before. The professor knew that the only reason he kept flying was because of how much he loved it.

This time felt different to the professor. He could hear the seriousness in Cody's voice. He thought that maybe this time, Cody had finally had enough.

So he said, "Okay, Cody, but as we discussed earlier, I think we should stop flying for the season. Because I'll tell you now, I think it's a bad idea."

Aside from Cody, the crash had been unsettling for everyone. Sally, Ryan, and the professor all talked about how they should maybe quit for the season as the regular winds were beginning to pick up even more.

The moment they had brought it up with Cody, though, he had shut them down immediately. This time was no different.

"I know you don't want me to do it, but I'm telling you, this is what I need."

The professor took a moment to consider before caving in.

"Alright, Cody. If you want one more flight and you want to keep it private, it's alright with me. I can have everything ready in a week."

Cody's voice changed just enough to make the professor feel even more suspicious. "Perfect. That should be all I need. Thanks, Prof. I'll send you a location and let you know more in a week."

He hung up.

Later that day, Cody was at the gym with Ryan on their normal schedule. Ryan could tell something was off from the get-go. Where Cody would normally lift ninety pounds, he was only asking for seventy-five. Where he would normally push for fifteen reps, he only did ten.

Ryan figured that Cody was having an off day and tried to think nothing of it. He managed to do so until the end of the workout when Cody was laughing and more light-hearted than Ryan had seen him in the past couple of months.

"What's going on, Cody?" he finally asked after trying to hold back for so long.

Cody smiled and tried to shrug it off as if there was nothing to hide. "I don't know what you're talking about."

"Come on, cut the crap. You haven't laughed like this in ages. You're not trying today. It's like you've given up. If that's what makes you happy, let's quit today's workout."

Ryan had wanted Cody to stop flying ages ago. He could see how much it was tearing away at his body, his relationship with his wife, and the time Thomas craved to spend with him.

But every time he brought it up, Cody just got upset. He reminded Ryan that this was all he could do now that he couldn't ride his bike and struggled to get up out of a chair alone.

The flying had been the first thing to come between their friendship, and Ryan had had enough of it.

This time, Ryan wanted a straight answer out of Cody and wasn't going to drop it easily.

"Listen, man. You know I love you and that I would do anything in the world for you. But this is destroying you, and I can see it. Sally and Thomas miss you at home, and I can't stand the sad look on your face all the time."

Cody just sat still, staring straight ahead.

"Today, you've been different. All I want to know is what's going on. If there's something I need to look out for, then I have to know. Sally asks me all the time to look out for you, and that's what I'm trying to do.

At that, Cody snapped. "Listen! I can take care of myself. I know I may look all pathetic, but I can handle it. It's my body and my life. Sally can take it up with me; she doesn't need to put you in charge of it like you're my nanny."

It was the second time since Cody's big accident that he'd turned on Ryan like that. Two times more than he'd ever done in the two decades they'd been friends before that.

Ryan took a deep breath. The silence between the two of them felt infinite as each of them could feel the distance growing.

In the silence, neither of them knew exactly what to say, so they got up, Ryan helped Cody into his wheelchair, and they moved out to Ryan's car.

The two of them went through the well-practiced motions of lifting Cody onto the passenger's seat, folding the wheelchair, and cramming it into the back between all of Ryan's other ranger gear.

"I don't know if you blame me for what happened to you, Cody, but I'm sorry. I'm sorry I couldn't outride that bear. It's my fault you're stuck in that chair and that you'll never ride again, and I owe it to you to make sure you stay safe. I can't live with myself if I don't take care of what I've gone and messed up."

He broke into tears in the driver's seat with his head in his hands.

Cody hesitated at first but reached out and put his hand on Ryan's shoulder. When Ryan looked up, surprised, he held tight onto Cody's arm.

In the quiet, Cody quietly said, "It's not your fault, Ryan."

"It's my fault, and I've known that for a long time," was all that Ryan could get out.

Cody didn't want to let Ryan keep believing this, so he had to fight him further. "No, and I won't let you think that. It's my own fault. If I had just taken us down another trail, waited a bit longer, or done anything differently, I wouldn't be sitting here right now."

After another short pause, Cody continued on. "This all is my fault. Or it's at least that damn bear's fault. Either way, it's not yours. You saved my life. Without you, Thomas wouldn't even have a dad along for the ride, and I can't let you keep beating yourself down for it."

Cody decided that he needed to tell Ryan about his flight. He wanted Ryan to understand why he was going to go out and do this personal flight. In truth, he just wanted to scheme with his old friend again and plan a crazy wild adventure one last time.

He took a risk and told Ryan almost everything.

"Before I tell you, I want you to agree that you're not going to try and stop me. This is something I have to do, and I know it's dangerous. Regardless, I need your support on this, not your disappointed lack of approval. Can you do that?"

Ryan looked incredibly unsure, but he knew his friend well enough to realize that Cody needed him at that moment. He nodded his head and listened to Cody lay out one more wild plan like they used to when they were younger.

"There's an island, just about 25 miles off the coast, west of the national park. The park ends at the bluff line that's a couple hundred feet up above the water. I'm pretty sure that I can fly the distance, use the thermals to lift myself up like birds do, and get to the island in just over two hours."

He pulled out his phone and laid it on the middle compartment of the car, showing Ryan the map of the route he had already drawn on the GPS app they once used to find new trails to bike back in the day.

Looking at the map, Ryan tried to take it in and imagine if it was possible. "Cody, you've only flown for like thirty minutes before. What makes you think you can handle over two hours of continuous flight? You'll barely make it a couple miles, and then you'll definitely drown."

"But before now, I wasn't utilizing thermals. Plus, most of the time, I'll be coasting rather than actually propelling myself. I should be able to pick up a good speed and not actually have to exert too much energy. It's more akin to paragliding, but I can add the lift in when I need to."

The two of them looked at the map and the route that Cody had planned. He switched over to a map of the wind trends in that region, generally showing that the westerly winds would be pushing against him, but the winds that turned south could actually help him if he flew on a diagonal.

Ryan had to admit that this was a decently well-planned idea, but he still didn't know how to fully accept what seemed like a complete suicide mission coming from his best friend.

"This isn't me telling you not to do it, but this is nuts. You've thought it out, but I feel like it's going against physics and the capability of the human body. If you need to do it, I'll keep helping you train, but I can't say I'm fully behind this crazy idea."

Cody nodded. "I know. But I just needed you to know what my plan is anyway. I know that it could go wrong, but what's the point of living if I'm not going to push myself?"

It seemed like Ryan wasn't going to push him anymore.

"What do you need from me, then?" Ryan asked.

"All I need is your word that you won't say anything to Sally or Thomas and a ride to the bank."

With that, they headed off to the local bank where both of the boys had opened their first accounts, never moving their money elsewhere.

Ryan helped Cody out of the car and let him go inside by himself to take care of whatever he was doing while he stood next to the car, trying to understand the plan that Cody had just laid out in front of him.

As he was standing there, he noticed a few news vans that seemed to have recognized Cody outside the bank. After five minutes, two more had shown up, one from a local news station that Ryan remembered covering the first race he had ever won, likely because Cody had been sick that day. They sat there and waited for Cody to roll out of the bank doors.

After a while, Ryan decided to poke his head inside and see what was taking so long.

When he stepped in and was blasted by the air conditioning, he spotted Cody at the desk of Mr. Kollar, their primary school math teacher who had later switched careers and started working as a financial accountant.

Ryan gave him a wave, but Cody turned from him quickly as if trying to hide what they were doing.

Cody and Mr. Kollar shook hands after he had signed the multiple documents that Ryan had gotten inside in time to witness, and Cody made his way back toward the door.

He didn't mention what exactly he was doing inside, so Ryan didn't ask. He assumed it was something routine, never thinking about what else he could have been doing.

They headed outside into the downtown district and were instantly swamped by reporters. Apparently, even more had pulled up since Ryan had gone inside.

They were shouting questions at Cody, shooting picture after picture, and trying to get a response from him. Amidst the noise, Cody could hardly hear any of the questions, let alone answer them, so they pushed through the crowd and tried to get to the car.

Once they were at the car, Cody turned around and thanked everyone for their support but let them know that he wasn't going to be flying again anytime soon. There wasn't enough time left in the season, but he hoped to get out again next year right when the weather was good enough.

Cody was smart enough to know that the fanaticism over his flights was going to die down, but unlike the trees in spring, he doubted it would come back to life.

That was how most of these things happened. The first time it happened, people wanted to be there to see it. Now that it had already happened, people would forget about him soon enough. It wasn't like there were races in the sky that he could start to excel at. His time in the spotlight was over, and he knew that.

Instead, he spent all his time planning his own private flight with Ryan's help. They chose a day within the week because the weather window was closing quickly.

When Ryan dropped Cody off at home, Thomas was outside riding his bike and raced up to the car to greet them.

Before getting out of the car, Cody reminded Ryan of what they'd talked about. "Remember. Not a word. Please, Ryan. I can't have them talking me out of what I have to do."

Ryan just clapped Cody on the back and told him, "Not a word. Not to anyone."

They got out of the car, and Ryan declined a dinner invitation and drove off once Cody was settled into his chair and Sally had come out to say a quick hello.

Inside, Cody was back to his old self. He was laughing and playing with Thomas and even suggested a game of Uno, which he hadn't had the patience for since his accident.

Uno turned into "52 Card Pick Up," which turned into everyone on the ground wrestling and laughing as Sally and Cody took turns tickling Thomas.

Only once they were all barely able to keep moving did they quiet down and throw a movie on the TV.

Thomas was asleep almost instantly, as was Cody.

Sally, on the other hand, was wide awake. She was completely perplexed by how Cody was acting. While it was refreshing, she didn't understand what was going on.

She watched him sleep softly, cuddled up next to his son. She took her time noticing the little similarities between the two of them, like the weird dimple on their right cheeks that only showed up when they slept, the sudden movements like those of a small puppy while dreaming, and the soft breathing that eventually calmed Sally enough to fall asleep herself.

CHAPTER FIFTEEN

This happier, carefree Cody lasted several days, and he realized that they were some of the best days since his big accident. He felt at peace with everything that had happened and, more importantly, with the decision he had made about his final flight.

He spent those days playing with Thomas, training lightly with Ryan, and sitting in the forest with Sally for hours on end. He wanted to soak it all up before attempting a flight that he knew was impossible, a flight that he knew he wouldn't come back from.

When Ryan had expressed his concerns about the 25-mile flight, Cody had shrugged it off, reassuring him that he knew how to fly through the thermals and make it even easier on himself. In reality, Cody had known there was no way he would make it from the moment he decided to do the flight.

When the final morning came around for him to spend at home, he took it all in and tried to be grateful for the life he had built around himself. He thought about his dad, knowing he would have been proud of him for the life he had formed with Sally and Thomas. Cody had spent every waking moment of his life trying to act in ways that Rex would have smiled down on.

As he had for weeks, he considered again what his dad would have thought about what he was about to do. That thought made him shake his head and finally roll out of bed.

Today was the day that he would set out, without Sally knowing, for his final flight.

He carried himself over to his wheelchair and headed down the ramp into the kitchen. He moved slowly and deliberately, hand-grinding coffee beans as he boiled water. Each moment he would find himself appreciative of the smallest things.

The smell of fresh coffee was the first thing to begin poking at his brain, forcing him to wonder if this was the right move after all. Again, he shook the thought from his head and moved forward.

Just after he had thrown a few snacks into a bag and finished brewing coffee, he heard Ryan's Jeep pull up in the driveway.

Before Sally could wake up and ask what was going on, he rolled his way out the front door. Ryan helped him up into the Jeep, and they were off to the coastline.

Surprisingly, Ryan kept the drive lighthearted, and he didn't question Cody about his flight. They entered and drove through the national park, still empty in the early hour, until they reached the edge.

A massive sandstone bluff towered in front of them. There was a dirt track that led up the side, which was one of the reasons Cody told Ryan about the flight in the first place. He needed help getting up there, and Ryan's Jeep had taken on far worse back when they were scouting for new bike trails.

At the base of the dirt track, to Cody's relief, the professor had stored the wingsuit in a waterproof trunk, just as he had asked. Ryan hopped out and threw the trunk in the back of the Jeep, and they started up the bumpy road.

The drive up took a long time, but Cody still felt like he wasn't fully ready by the time Ryan began helping him get strapped into the wingsuit.

His nerves had come and gone with every flight, but now they were the strongest he had felt in a long time. His determination to fight the nerves wavered, but he continued to push his thoughts aside.

Once he was fully set up, he turned to Ryan to say goodbye, even if Ryan didn't know that was what it was.

"Ryan, I don't think you know how much I love you. I could never have gotten back out of the hole I was in if you weren't there every step of the way."

Ryan laughed and knocked Cody's shoulder. "Hey now, you don't need to get sappy. I'll see you in a few hours."

"Well, yeah, but just in case anything goes wrong, I want it to be you that takes Thomas in. I think you know that, but I need it to be clear."

"Are you sure you need to take this flight? Take the risk?" Cody's words were leaving Ryan unsure of what exactly they were doing up on that bluff.

Cody shrugged and nodded dismissively. "This is just what I need to do. I don't think I have any other choice."

"Well, you know I support you no matter what. Fly true out there, Long Legs."

Cody laughed at that and said, "Haven't heard that one in a long time, huh? People must have thought my legs had just gone away." He looked down and feigned surprise to see his legs missing.

The two of them shared a last laugh over a bad joke before hugging each other.

With that, Cody launched himself down the hill.

He picked up speed, keeping himself as aerodynamic as possible until he had enough speed to extend his wings and take off into the air.

Within seconds he was out above the coastline with nothing but hundreds of feet of air below him.

The compass he had fasted to his wrist pointed him in the right direction, and he set off. His body felt strong, and his mind felt calm as he set out on his final flight.

Cody went into autopilot and started thinking back on everything that led him to this decision.

Since the accident, Cody's life had been fully reliant upon others. He could barely get out of bed in the morning without Sally's help, let alone make it in and out of the bathroom anymore.

Back when he was racing bikes, he was at his prime. He was on top of the world, speeding down courses people had designed just to challenge riders like him. Breaking those puzzles and leading the downhill charge was what he lived for.

Bringing Thomas into the world had been the only thing to come close to the thrill he got from riding, but as Thomas got older, he would want someone that could ride bikes and go on long trips with him. In a way, Cody had to watch Ryan be more of a father figure to Thomas over the last year.

Even Sally treated him differently now. She was more hesitant to trust him with tasks around the house, and she barely ever left him alone without fearing that something would go wrong.

His reliance on others had been cutting away at him for months. The lack of independence made it feel as if he wasn't even living his own life anymore.

Flying was the only time he felt he could still reclaim his independence. He was all alone up in the air, the only one fully in control of what was going on. No one needed to help him once he was off the ground.

But he also knew that his time spent in the air was coming to an end. That feeling of euphoria and freedom was fading, and Cody couldn't contemplate what a winter spent stuck inside would be like. He couldn't face his own insecurities, knowing he would depend upon everyone to help him get through a daily routine.

All of those feelings had led him to this point.

Cody knew there was no way he was making it to that tiny little island far off the coast. That island only represented an unreachable goal, the independent life he once had but could never reach again.

He only wanted one last flight, one last feeling of pure freedom, before finally taking himself out of the pain that had been constant since the accident.

Lost in his thoughts, Cody continued to adjust his flight path in the direction of the island.

Something inside him was still steering him toward that unattainable goal.

Out of nowhere, a strong thermal current took hold of Cody and his wingsuit, thrusting him upward. The strength of the movement lurched Cody forward in his harness, completely unbalancing the system.

The awkward weight distribution tipped Cody to one side, and he immediately began to plummet.

He watched as the ocean rushed toward him but continued to fight, trying to readjust his weight so he could get some air back under his wings.

With a final thrust of his hips, he was able to shift just enough to bring control back to his arms. He executed a series of powerful motions that lifted him into the air but left him feeling weak.

As he continued to fight against gravity, he considered why he was even fighting to stay in the air. Wasn't this what he was expecting? He was so sure that he hadn't wanted to return from this flight, but his instincts continued to force him up.

He followed that instinct, righted his course, and continued to push forward. Something inside him wasn't ready to let go just yet.

****

At the McCully house, Sally had woken up to realize Cody was nowhere to be found. She had learned to stop listening to her anxious feelings as Cody seemed to cheer up over the last few days, but now all those feelings rushed in at once.

She ran into Thomas's room and woke him up to take him out into the car.

The two of them set off down the road, dirt and gravel flying up behind them. Thomas hooted and hollered in excitement, unable to sense the urgency and stress behind the wild driving.

Sally pulled into Ryan's driveway, but as soon as she saw that the Jeep was gone, she knew he had something to do with Cody's absence.

She pulled out her phone and dialed Ryan immediately.

"Hello?" At least he had answered, but Sally could hear the hesitancy behind his voice.

"Where are you? Where's Cody? I can't shake the feeling of something being totally wrong right now, and I woke up to Cody missing. What's happening, Ryan?"

When Sally got upset, everyone knew they didn't have much of a choice but to answer her and hope she was able to calm down and forgive them. It didn't help that it was hard to hear her over the strong winds of the bluff line that Ryan still stood on.

"Okay, I know. But he's alright. Well, I think he is. Listen, Sally, He asked me not to say anything. He told me you'd freak out about his flight."

Freak out is exactly what she did.

"His flight?! What do you mean, his flight? Where are you guys?"

Ryan took a long look out over the ocean. Cody had disappeared from sight a long time ago, but he still couldn't get himself to move from that spot.

At that, Ryan broke and told her absolutely everything, starting from the first day that Cody had proposed the idea and asked for his help.

****

Over an hour and a half into the flight, Cody's body was as tired as it had ever been. He was pushing himself far past his capability but still refused to give up.

He had hit a few thermal chutes that helped him get back up higher in the air and have a few moments of rest from coasting along. Even those rests felt incredibly demanding rather than like an actual break.

But still, he pushed on.

Memories of his family and friends began to pour in.

He saw Sally at the altar, the woman he loved more than anything in this world. He had spent almost his entire life with her, having teased her all the way back in the first grade. They had walked hand in hand through everything that came at them.

Then he watched on as Thomas came into the world. He could almost feel the feeling of holding his son for the first time. Memories of Thomas growing up flooded his mind. From teaching him how to ride a bike to taking him up in his old childhood treehouse at Cody's mom's house, every memory jolted Cody into pushing harder.

Then there was Ryan. What he had told him back on the bluff was fully true. He didn't have any idea of how he would still be here without that man and everything he had done for his family. There was no real need for him to do any of what he had for them, but he had been there through the darkest of all days.

The image of his father came to the forefront of his mind – the days he spent with his mom and dad, building a treehouse, running around the yard, learning bird calls, visiting the ranger station, and all the other moments that were defined by his parents and their love for him.

He could feel the love from these people so strongly at that moment. It was the only thing that kept him moving.

All of Cody's thoughts about his past mountain biking days and the things he could do when he had full control of his legs were far from his mind.

Being able to ride a bike wasn't all that life was about.

The freedom that came with riding a bike or flying was all he had been seeking, but it was far from what mattered the most.

The memories that came back to him weren't about the small day-to-day events, nor were they about the big milestones. He had won countless biking medals and been the first to fly through the air with his own power, but that didn't matter.

Every single memory that popped up was about his family and friends.

At that moment, he realized something that had been escaping him for the last year.

Life isn't about having big, grand accomplishments or being successful. It's about forming and cherishing the memories of love between himself and his family and friends. Cody finally realized that love is the only thing that matters, that is remembered.

We are born from dust and return to dust. The only thing we carry with us is the love created during the short time in between.

Cody realized that he couldn't just give up. He had been focused on the wrong things his entire life.

He didn't want to die. He wanted to live. He wanted to love.

Immediately he began to panic, looking for a nearby island he could change his course toward.

But there was nothing in sight aside from the one island far in the distance. He knew he had at least two miles to go. Coasting at his current height, he could only go for about another mile, and there wasn't an ounce of energy left in his body to make it any further.

There was nothing left for him to do but coast and hope that a thermal updraft would take him higher.

Although Cody felt driven by the powerful memories of the vast love he had in his life, he was still zapped of energy. He barely made it another thousand yards before he started rapidly descending toward the vast openness of the ocean.

Then he hit. Water enveloped him as he struggled to fight his way free of the wingsuit.

CHAPTER SIXTEEN

Thomas sat in the back of the car, oblivious to what was going on. He sensed the immense stress coming from his mom, but he didn't know what was causing it. He had never seen his mom drive this fast before, and it would have been fun if he didn't have so much on his mind.

He remembered his dad telling him stories about his grandfather. Although he had never met him, he knew all about the kind of man he was, a brave, kind, adventurous, hardworking person who always gave love to everyone.

His dad had also told him the story of how his grandfather had died, the tragic day he was out in his car searching for Cody. It was a story that Thomas took caution from. He never wanted to lose his own father, so he never did anything that could put his dad at risk.

From the way his mom was acting right now, there seemed to be a chance that his dad was in trouble, so he listened, rode along, and stayed quiet.

After what felt like days, they pulled up to the docks underneath a giant Coast Guard sign. Ryan was already there, and Thomas watched his mom sprint past Ryan and straight into the main office.

She was only inside for a minute before a team came out the door with his mom right behind them. He could vaguely hear Sally shout something over to Ryan, who had been standing and waiting with Thomas.

The two of them hurried to catch up to his mom and the rescue team, jumping onto a small Coast Guard boat that was tethered to the first slip of the dock.

The boat engine started up, and Thomas was immediately overwhelmed by the whirring of the motor and the smell of salt water mixed with diesel fuel.

Everyone else was standing toward the front of the boat, scanning the water and the skies. Ryan was attempting to draw out a path through the sky toward what looked like a small island far off in the distance.

The boat cut through the waves toward the small island that slowly grew as they neared it.

By this point, Thomas understood that they were looking for his dad. He didn't know why he would be out in the middle of the ocean like this but assumed he should help.

He stood up and started looking out from the boat until one of the rescue team members urged him back to his seat.

There were a few signs of whales in the ocean and dozens of seabirds scattered through the sky, but there was nothing that looked remotely like a large man-bird flying through the air. Despite the empty skies, they were still hopeful they would find Cody and kept moving toward the island.

Just as the boat was starting to slow down to make its way around some of the smaller pieces of land spreading out from the main island, Thomas saw a disturbance in the water.

It was only a few hundred feet away from the boat, but it didn't seem like anyone else saw it.

He had stayed quiet this entire time, but there was no way he was going to rely on these strangers to find his dad. Cody had done that, and his father hadn't made it home.

"There! Over there! Turn to the right!!" Thomas shouted out.

The Coast Guard's immediate reaction was to ignore him, writing it off as the imagination of a child. Then one of them saw what Thomas was pointing out and gave the orders to veer starboard.

As soon as they turned starboard, everyone realized that the disturbance in the water was, in fact, Cody and that he was tangled up in the wings and his head was barely breaking the surface of the water.

Cody had heard the distant sound of a boat engine and had hoped that, by some miracle, the people on the boat had seen him and were on their way, but he had already been in the cold water for at least 45 minutes trying to free himself loose from the wings. He had no energy to call for help or even look in the direction of the boat, though he did get one final burst of adrenaline in his attempt to stay afloat when he realized the sound of the boat was heading in his direction.

However, though Cody knew that the approaching boat was only seconds away, it didn't matter; he was done. Cody knew his time on the planet was finished. He accepted his fate and let his body begin its descent toward the dark and cold ocean floor.

As the rescue boat was racing toward what they now could tell was Cody and his wingsuit, they were momentarily elated to see that he was still alive and fighting to stay above water. That feeling quickly changed to urgency and concern as they saw Cody stop moving and begin to sink below the surface of the water. Upon reaching the area where Cody was last seen, Ryan and one of the Coast Guard members reached over the side of the boat and were somehow able to grab a piece of the wingsuit and pull it up, along with Cody.

With the help of the other two Coast Guard members, they hauled Cody out of the water, wingsuit and all, over the gunwales and into the boat.

Thomas saw his dad lying there, seemingly lifeless.

He began screaming as tears streamed from his eyes, assuming he had lost his dad to the sea and a failed attempt at an unimaginable flight.

Ryan and Sally worked quickly to rip the wingsuit free from Cody's body while the Coast Guard members gave him CPR compressions and forced air into his lungs with their handheld breathing device.

It was nothing like Thomas had seen in the movies. His mom watched in disbelief while the Coast Guard continued pressing hard on what could have been a dummy.

Thomas forced himself to look away toward the island his dad had crash-landed so near to. His mind was racing; his world was going dark.

The coughing and sputtering coming from behind yanked him back to reality. He turned and saw his dad on his side, breathing.

Thomas ran to him and threw himself on top of him. While Ryan and Sally tried to tell him to be careful, Cody's arms reached up and pulled Thomas even closer.

Still coughing and spitting up some water, Cody leaned into Thomas and whispered to him, "Thomas, I'm so sorry. I swear I will never leave you again, no matter what the world brings us. I'm here, and I'm going to stay right here for the rest of my life."

Thomas, with tears still running down his face, smiled and pointed toward the nearby island.

"Dad. Look! You almost made it!"

Cody forced himself to sit up and look.

The island was nearly a quarter mile away, but it wasn't the island that grabbed his attention.

He saw the last bits of the wingsuit, the last parts of the contraption that had given him a chance to live again but had also convinced him to stop living.

Cody smiled and turned away from the sight to look back at his family, the only thing that really mattered from the very beginning to the end.

THE END

9 798868 921834